Timpson's

Norfolk

Notebook

**A personal survey
of a rather special
county**

John Timpson

Acorn Publishing

Published by Acorn Publishing
The Old County School
Northgate Street
Bury St Edmunds
Suffolk IP33 1HP

A CIP catalogue record for this book is available from the British Library.

ISBN 1 903592 00 3

Printed in Great Britain by Ashford Colour Press.

Contents

CHAPTER TWO
Remarkable Norfolk people: Prizefighters, bodysnatchers and inventors...

CHAPTER THREE
Places with strange tales to tell: A bridge, a garden, an abbey...

CHAPTER FOUR
Legends and traditions: Some are just memories, others still live on

Introduction

WHEN WE FIRST MOVED TO Norfolk as newly-weds, exactly half a century ago, our families and friends thought we were quite mad. To them, East Anglia was just a boring bulge on the backside of Britain, a flat expanse of nothing in particular except for the occasional windmill and permanently swept by Arctic winds, a cross between Siberia and the Zuider Zee.

I confess I had much the same picture. My two previous excursions to Norfolk had not been auspicious. One was a family holiday with my parents in Cromer, when it rained continuously and the only entertainment was watching the fire brigade pump out the hotel basement. The other was as a National Serviceman during the bitter winter of 1947, when predictably the Army ran out of fuel and we could only warm our hut by burning the chairs, the tables, and even the spare beds. We were working our way through the roof joists when we were finally dispatched to the comparatively tropical climes of the Austrian Alps. I often wonder how our successors fared in that ill-fated hut – and which collapsed first, them or the roof.

It was the offer of a reporting job in Dereham that brought me back. Alas, the weather had not improved. There was rarely a winter when the lanes were not blocked, and in our pantry the pickled onions froze in the vinegar and the eggs solidified and burst their shells. Our sanitation system was a bucket down the garden emptied by the 'night soil men' – who always came at breakfast time, providing an exotic aroma to the bacon and eggs. The water supply was hand-pumped from a well by the back door, and on washdays we lit a fire under the copper in the wash-house to heat the water. We stepped back into the living conditions of the 19th century, and into a society that was not exactly feudal, but older folk were still tempted to touch their forelocks as the squire rode by.

Nevertheless, during those early years in North Elmham we developed an affection for Norfolk which has stayed with us ever since. We discovered that once you get to know a Norfolkman, there is no better friend; once you get to know Norfolk, there is no better place to live.

When the London job with the BBC came along in 1959 and we reluctantly went back 'down south', we kept in touch with our Norfolk friends, we came back as often as we could, and I shamelessly extolled the delights of Norfolk whenever the opportunity arose – much to the irritation, I suspect, of my fellow broadcasters. For nearly three decades, as the home Counties became more and more congested and the daily battle with the London rat-race became more and more tedious, we promised ourselves that one day we would return to Norfolk – permanently. Not every daydream materialises, but happily this was one that did.

The builder who worked on our cottage before we moved back gave me a refreshing reminder of the different world to which we were returning. I came up one weekend to find that nothing much had happened since the weekend before. A little impatiently, I fear, I asked him how things were going.

There was a considerable pause while he surveyed the apparent muddle around us – the heaps of rubble, the trampled mud, the half-built walls and the tile-less roof. Then he nodded gently. 'Why,' he said, 'thass comin' t'gether.'

And sure enough, in due course, it did.

Fifteen years later we are still good friends, and during that time I have learnt quite a lot more about the sometimes quirky features of Norfolk and Norfolk life. In spite of all the inevitable changes that have taken place, the essential character of this rather special county still survives. I shall never know it as well as a Norfolkman does but perhaps I can appreciate it just as much, in a different way, from an incomer's point of view.

In this Norfolk Notebook, to borrow a description of my other books, I have tried to look beyond the obvious for the unusual, the unlikely and the definitely odd. In the first chapter for instance, on the Norfolk countryside, I could hardly ignore all those medieval churches but I have looked at some of the surprises they contain rather than the grandeur of their architecture. No Norfolk calendar would be complete without a windmill, but I am just as taken with Norfolk's dovecotes and the 17th century Norfolk squire who wrote a manual on how to build them. And while we are used to seeing golden corn and bright yellow rape, how about those fields of blue lavender at Heacham and the rather less fragrant coprolite they used to gather at West Dereham – better known as dinosaurs, dung!

The section on remarkable Norfolk people makes only a passing reference, I am afraid, to the man who is featured on so many pub signs as 'The Norfolk Hero'; I think Lord Nelson comes under the heading of 'obvious'. So I have turned to another Norfolk naval hero, only recently honoured in his own county but with towns and islands named after him elsewhere, Captain George Vancouver. Norfolk had its heroic women too, not only the famous Queen Boudicca but also, for instance, the squire,s wife who defended his castle with twelve men against a force of a thousand.

While Norfolk is proud that Abraham Lincoln's ancestors came from here, the descendants of other local emigrants made an impact too, including a Townshend who put a massive chain across the Hudson River to halt English ships during the War of Independence. Incidentally, he was a kinsman of the Townshend of Raynham Hall who, as Chancellor, imposed the colonial tax which virtually started the war.

Then there are 'ordinary', places in Norfolk with strange tales to tell, from the pub which has a Bible in the bar, presented by an over-optimistic curate, to the old barn which has effigies on the roof commemorating a feud between the farmer and the lord of the manor. There is even a 14th century church which was moved, piece-by-piece, by a Victorian parson to a more convenient central position. Only the original tower was left behind on the old site a mile away.

In the final section there are some of the legends and traditions which enrich Norfolk's history. Some are well-documented and still maintained, famous ones like the Bishop,s annual wherry trip to St Benet's Abbey in his unique double role as Abbot, more localised ones like the church parade of the elderly ladies of Castle Rising's 17th century 'hospital', wearing their scarlet cloaks and tall pointed hats, and led by the matron in an even grander cloak with a three-tiered cape and a dashing tricorn hat trimmed with an ostrich feather.

The evidence for other unusual aspects of Norfolk's past is sometimes flimsier. Did Bromholm Priory really acquire a piece of the True Cross which could work miracles? Did Robert Kett really assemble his rebels under all those Kett's Oaks? And I wonder if there really was a well at Happisburgh haunted by a legless smuggler – not just drunk, his legs were chopped off by his murderers. Never mind, I am sure they all have an element of truth and they all add to the flavour of Norfolk.

There is one other facet of life in this very special county which is not only unique but quite literally inimitable. I rarely attempt it – and never in the presence of a Norfolkman! It is risky for an incomer even to try reproducing it on paper, but no Norfolk notebook would be complete without at least a modest sample of the Norfolk dialect, which in spite of progress has lived on through the centuries, and I hope will continue to do so. May I say then, with apologies to all my Norfolk-born friends!

'Fare y'well t'gether…'

John Timpson

Chapter one

The Norfolk landscape: Mermaids, angels and a flamingo…

Beyond the Great Ouse

Why Walsoken was so often soken, and the search for Ongar Hill

WHEN NORFOLK GETS ITS ANNUAL influx of summer holidaymakers I have been known to wax lyrical about the deserted beaches that lie along the north Norfolk coast, away from the main resorts. On a fine summer's day, while the holiday beaches are packed, it has been possible to walk out beyond the salt marshes at places like Titchwell or Holme-next-the-Sea, and find yourself on a vast expanse of empty sand, with not a soul in any direction – just the seabirds, sand-dunes and sea.

Alas, over the years these isolated corners have been discovered by a wider public – perhaps because of the indiscreet eulogies of people like myself. Titchwell is now an official bird sanctuary, which is fine for the birds but not so good for the non-birdwatcher, ducking under telescopic lenses and tripping over tripods on the path down to the beach; and Holme-next-the-Sea is now near the junction of two much-publicised long-distance footpaths, so seekers of solitude can no longer say there is no place like Holme.

Not that these beaches are exactly congested. There is still plenty of room for a full-scale cricket match without disturbing any sunbathers, and you can safely snooze among the sand dunes without being trampled underfoot. But for those who regard even a distant figure on the horizon as an infringement of their privacy, the halcyon days of undisturbed isolation would seem to be over.

Except at Ongar Hill...

When I first came to Norfolk many years ago, I assumed that the county ended at King's Lynn. The Great Ouse seemed to provide a natural boundary, and with the Little Ouse and the Waveney cutting us off from Suffolk in the south, and the sea on the other two sides, I cherished the thought that Norfolk was actually an off-shore island.

But of course it extends beyond the Great Ouse, almost as far as Sutton Bridge. This is the part of the county which Noel Coward must have been referring to in his famous put-down: 'Very Flat, Norfolk.' From Welney to Walpole Cross Keys, from the Wiggenhalls to Walsoken, flatness abounds. It is not the sort of landscape to tempt the average holidaymaker, and most of them hasten through it to enjoy the companionship of the Hardwick roundabout at King's Lynn. It would not occur to them to turn off the A17 at Terrington St Clement or Clenchwarton, and venture into the confusing maze of lanes which apparently lead through nothingness into nowhere, but which actually end at Ongar Hill.

Hans Verkroost © Acorn Magazines

Great Ouse – King's Lynn

The name is rather misleading. This remote little settlement is nothing like that other Ongar, 100 miles away in Essex at the end of the Central Line, and if there was ever a hill at Ongar Hill, it is certainly not there now.

The lane that leads to it takes you beyond the ancient sea bank that used to protect Terrington – not always successfully – and across Terrington Marsh, which until the last century really was a marsh. It is shown as such on Faden's famous map, published in 1797, and the lane skirting round the edge of it, along an embankment, petered out at what was then called Hungry Hill. Presumably Hungry became Hunger, and Hunger became Ongar; but what could have happened to the hill?

These days Terrington Marsh, like the rest of Norfolk's marshland, is one of the most fertile areas in Britain, but it is still one of the emptiest. There are vast fields of wheat and potatoes and barley, isolated cottages, the occasional farmhouse and little side turnings that lead to nowhere. Even on a sunny summer's day it all has a certain eeriness; there is always the thought that a couple of centuries ago you would have been in an enormous bog, and in earlier times you would have been under the sea.

At the end of the Ice Age the Wash extended 30 miles inland, submerging Wisbech and lapping around Peterborough. By the time the Romans came the area was mostly marsh, regularly flooded by the sea to the east and the rivers to the west. Whether it was freshwater or seawater, the effect was equally unpleasant.

Medieval farmers built embankments to protect their villages; they put the 'Wal' in places like the Walpoles and the Waltons. But the floods often won and at Walsoken, for instance, in spite of their wall the villagers were still, as it were, 'soken'. At Terrington St Clement they were still having problems in the 17th century, when the sea breached the embankment and the villagers had to take refuge in the church tower until the waters subsided, with supplies being brought by boat from King's Lynn.

Looking back across Terrington Marsh from Ongar Hill it is difficult to visualise how a flood could reach that far, across the miles of fields, particularly as Ongar Hill itself is now a quarter-of-a-mile inland. The lane runs out at the old sea wall that used to protect it, where a couple of coastguards' cottages still stand. Beyond it are more flat fields, reclaimed in 1775 when yet another sea wall was built beyond them.

The farmers have taken over, and the coastguards have moved to somewhere a little closer to the sea...

You have to leave your car by the cottages and follow a footpath out to the final sea wall – and here at last is isolation indeed. On each side the path along the top of the wall disappears into the distance, eventually to reach Sutton Bridge one way and King's Lynn the other. Behind you are the reclaimed fields: ahead is what they looked like before, a huge expanse of salt marsh and mud stretching away to the waters of the Wash.

The river channel of the Great Ouse passes through it, and you may see a distant yacht on its way from Lynn to the open water, just a white sail miraculously floating through the mud. But unless you are very unlucky, the path itself is deserted and you begin to feel like the last man left on earth.

But not quite the last. Even in this isolated corner, there is now an information board and a map, and although I met nobody, there was evidence that others had been there before – with their dogs. I viewed their leavings with much the same apprehension that Robinson Crusoe felt when he saw the solitary footprint in the sand...

I suppose it is possible, in due course, that this remote Norfolk outpost will be overrun by visitors, and an ice-cream van may lurk beside the coastguards' cottages; but somehow I doubt it. It is such an obscure location, so difficult to find, and in fact such a blank spot on the map, that I do not expect to meet too many coach parties on the road to Ongar Hill.

And beyond the Waveney

An extra corner of Norfolk where the Romans thought great forts!

THERE IS NO DOUBT ABOUT it, the county boundaries of Norfolk have their idiosyncrasies. In the west we have that extra slice of Norfolk on the far side of the Great Ouse, where you might reasonably expect Lincolnshire to begin. There is a similar illogicality about the boundary at the other extremity of the Norfolk coastline. From where the River Waveney rises in Lopham Fen, as far as St Olave's, it provides a natural boundary with Suffolk, and you might well assume that it would continue to do so along the rest of its course to Breydon Water and the sea. In fact it did, except for a last-minute detour around Gorleston, until someone waved a wand and made the boundary line veer away from the river and head off through Fritton Lake to Hopton-on-Sea.

So we now have this triangular wedge of Norfolk-beyond-the-Waveney, corresponding to the extra slice of Norfolk-beyond-the-Ouse. But their character could hardly be more different. In contrast to the deserted coastline of the Wash around Ongar Hill in the west, there are the holiday camps and caravan sites that follow the route along the coast of the A12, the busiest road in East Norfolk. It is only when you move inland that you leave behind the campers and the cars and discover one of Norfolk's most important ancient sites, which Suffolk must surely have been reluctant to lose; the ruins of the Roman fort of Gariannonum, now called Burgh Castle.

Needless to say, a Roman legionary would experience quite a shock if he were posted to Burgh Castle today. It is not only the change of name, though that is comprehensive enough. For once, the planners cannot be blamed. It happened soon after the Romans left Gariannonum and tribal groups took over East Anglia. The nearest group in the vicinity were called the Cnoveringas, a complicated exercise in spelling as well as pronunciation, and it is a simplified version of their name that lives on in the ancient Hundred of Clavering, in a loop of the Waveney. The Cnoveringas were Cno-fools and recognised the strategic position of the Roman fort. So they took it over, the experts tell us, and made it their own stronghold or 'burgh'. With their penchant for multi-syllables they christened it Cnobheresburg, but again posterity took an easier way out and left us with Burgh Castle.

Having got used to its name, the returning Roman legionary would then have to get used to the view, which has also totally changed. These days the fort is separated from Breydon Water by a broad stretch of marshland; in his day it overlooked a vast tidal estuary which completely covered the marshes, and instead of a few holiday craft there were war galleys at anchor and trading ships with goods destined for Caistor St Edmund, the Roman headquarters near Norwich.

The estuary was in fact a major naval base, perhaps the biggest on the east coast, and Gariannonum was one of the most important 'Forts of the Saxon Shore', built to defend the coastline against marauding Saxons from Germany. When the Romans moved out, the Saxons moved in, to become the North Folk of the East Angles. As for the great tidal estuary, over the centuries the tide went out – and never came back.

The other notable Fort of the Saxon Shore was at Branidonum, a name that escaped any wholesale re-adjustment by multi-syllabic tribes and is still recognisable as Brancaster. In this case, only the site of the fort remains. Today the Brancaster shoreline is garrisoned by golfers, hoping to preserve their greens from the inroads of the sea, and instead of a Roman fort, the clubhouse occupies a commanding position overlooking the sands. Brancaster still has its invaders, but they are armed with nothing more lethal – one hopes – than a bucket and spade. Of Branidonum itself, just the name on a road sign survives.

Gariannonum, on the other hand, is still an impressive sight. The ruins of three boundary walls still stand, enclosing an area of more than 600 feet long and nearly 400 feet wide. It was large enough to take a garrison of up to 1,000 men – including, at one time, an unlikely contingent of African cavalry. The Roman General who posted them there must have had a shaky knowledge of geography or a bizarre sense of humour.

On the far side of the estuary was the town and port of Caister, with only an 'e' instead of an 'o' to distinguish it from its namesake inland.

These days it's sometimes called Caister-by-Yarmouth to make the distinction clearer, but when the Romans were around, Yarmouth did not exist, and nor did the sandbank on which it stands. That only emerged as the estuary silted up, and Saxon fishermen moved onto it to land their catches. Presumably they were not the Cnoveringas, or we might be calling Yarmouth Cnobheresburg-on-Sea.

While Yarmouth was growing from a sandbank into a seaport, the original port of Caister was declining. The only reminders of its earlier importance are a few remnants of wall beside the coast road and a lonely Roman standing guard on the sign outside the Centurion pub. But on the other side of Breydon Water the ruins of Gariannonum still dominate the triangle of land that is Norfolk-beyond-the-Waveney.

Trying to follow the Icknield Way

The Romans got it straight – too straight –
then the ramblers re-invented it

I HAVE BECOME RATHER EXASPERATED with the Romans; they were far too good at building roads. I am also becoming the teeniest bit exasperated with the ramblers, because they are far too good at inventing new paths with old names. It can cause quite a problem if you are trying to trace the original steps taken by our forefathers, and one target for both the Romans and the ramblers has been the route that Neolithic man took from the Wiltshire plains to the Norfolk coast. It has been called England's oldest road; its name is the Icknield Way.

The Romans confused things with their passion for straight lines. The Icknield follows a chalk ridge between forest on the higher ground and marshes below, and when the chalk ridge curved, the Icknield curved too. But the Romans didn't fancy that at all and on several sections they 'Romanised' it, smoothing out the bends or building a new straight road alongside. Here in Norfolk, for instance, where the Icknield Way meanders gently from Thetford to Old Hunstanton, the Romans drew a straight line that we know as Peddars Way.

Then, to add to the problem, ramblers' associations and county council tourist departments decided that where the original Icknield Way is now a main road – the dual carriageway between Baldock and Royston is a good example – or where it is obliterated by places like Luton and Dunstable, they would invent a new route through the countryside and call it the Icknield Way Path. As a result they have diverted the Path – and goodness knows how many visitors – from one of Norfolk's most historic towns.

The original Icknield Way entered Norfolk at Nuns' Bridges in Thetford – though of course the bridges weren't there at the time. The Icknield Way Path heads off to the east, partly to avoid main roads, partly because of difficulties over rights of way, and partly to meet up conveniently both with the Peddars Way and a modern invention called the Angles Way, another long-distance path that was created less than a decade ago. I am glad to say that there were objections to the diversion of the Icknield Way within the organisation largely responsible for it, the Icknield Way Association; members have urged that the original route offers more of historical interest than the new one.

Just across the Nuns' Bridges, a massive earthworks – the largest in East Anglia and second only to Silbury Hill in Wiltshire, at the far end of the Icknield Way – provides evidence of a very early age. Its origins are obscure, but personally I favour the local legend that, after the Devil had dug his Dyke at Newmarket, he jumped to Thetford, spun round on one foot while deciding where to dig next, and created the earthworks with his heel. Maybe his next leap took him to Silbury Hill…

The experts are sceptical about this and argued among themselves for many years: some said the earthworks had been built by the Celts, others favoured the Romans, or the Saxons, or the Danes. Even Oliver Cromwell got a few votes. In the 1960's, however, excavations showed that the site had been occupied in the Iron Age. Centuries later, the Normans built a motte and bailey castle on the same site.

North of Thetford the Icknield Way disappears from the maps and Peddars Way takes over. However, I found a kindred spirit in Mr Bob Rose, of the Icknield Way Association, a great activist for restoring the Thetford route. He has worked out what he considers to be the true Icknield Way to Old Hunstanton and he has actually cycled along it.

Mr Rose's Icknield Way and the Peddars Way are virtually parallel, but the Icknield understandably weaves about a bit, so sometimes they are within sight of each other, sometimes a few miles apart.

He first cycled up the Peddars Way, then returned along his own route, via byways and bridleways that took him through Ringstead, Sedgeford, Flitcham, Gayton Thorpe and East Walton to Narford; that was on the first day. Next morning he continued to Cockley Cley, where the reconstructed Iceni village is a reminder that they may have originated the name of the Icknield Way, though it had already existed for three or four thousand years. At Hilborough the Way was blocked by the Stanford Battle Area, so he diverted through Ickburgh (another Icknield connection?) and rejoined the Way at Croxton, just north of Thetford. He wrote afterwards: 'I thoroughly enjoyed discovering for myself this relatively unexplored part of the Icknield Way, and I hope that others might also be so encouraged.'

Now it ought to be said that Mr Rose and the Romans were both probably right about the route of the Icknield Way, because it was not just a narrow path but a whole skein of parallel tracks, weaving about on the chalk ridge to avoid natural obstacles, and no doubt one track was easier in the summer, another in the winter. Both their routes could be within that broad swathe across West Norfolk. So if you find Peddars Way swarming with happy hikers all walking in a Roman straight line, I suggest you follow Mr Rose's example and have a peaceful meander along that other route where the Stone Age travellers trod. They weren't in a hurry either...

Famous forays into the fens

From Popham to Bellamy via Lady de Sodington Blount

IT WAS A PHOTOGRAPH OF David Bellamy lurking among the willows on the edge of the Fens, like some latter-day Hereward the Wake but twice as terrifying, that brought me up-to-date with a jolt from the world of Sir John Popham and Popham's Eau. It struck me that Sir John and Professor Bellamy both visited that south-western corner of Norfolk on similar missions, to introduce a new use for this flat and watery landscape.

I had just discovered that Popham's Eau, the channel linking the River Nene to Well Creek at Nordelph is not quite as boring as it looks. It is the only reminder we have of one of the earliest commercial attempts to drain the Fens; and in the course of reading about it I unearthed another extraordinary character connected with this remote area.

But first, Sir John Popham, Lord Chief Justice under James I, an eminent lawyer, a shrewd politician – and something of a speculator too. Sir John's speculative eye fell on the Fens, and his connections in high places did the rest.

He and his friends moved in on the Fens as 'adventurers' and 'undertakers'. They 'adventured' their money on draining the marshland, and 'undertook' to maintain the drainage system in good order, for all time. In return they were given a vast acreage of the drained land for their own use.

The locals, needless to say, were not consulted. They were told, either to hand over part of their land, or to pay towards the cost of drainage. That meant they lost the hunting and fishing grounds that provided their livelihood, and had to pay rates they could not afford for land they did not particularly want. Small wonder that among the Fenmen Sir John Popham's name was mud – albeit, well-drained mud.

Work started on Popham's Eau in 1605. It took a little time for local reaction to reach London, but in due course King James was warned that the 'covetous and Bloodie Popham', as he was popularly known in Norfolk, was bringing ruin to the Fenmen; 'he is cursed by all the poor in that part of England.' As a result, maybe the King had a quiet word with Sir John on the lines that the Lord Chief Justice was giving justice a bad name – or maybe it was the curse that did the trick. More likely, digging drains through bogs turned out to be a lot trickier than they expected. But three years later the scheme was abandoned. For Sir John and his fellow investors, Popham's Eau must have become known as Popham's Eau Dear…

The respite for the Fenmen was only brief. 'Adventurers' and 'undertakers' continued to try their luck elsewhere in the Fens, and thirty-odd years later, along came Cornelius Vermuyden and drained the lot. The bogs and marshes, no longer boggy or marshy, were put to new use as the most fertile farming land in Britain.

Exactly three hundred years after Popham tried to exploit the flat area around Nordelph and Upwell, its very flatness was put to a rather different use by a remarkable lady called Lady Elizabeth de Sodington Blount, whose name alone is worth recording for posterity, let alone the eccentric activities of the lady herself. Lady Blount headed the Universal Zetetic Society, dedicated to the unshakeable belief that the earth was flat. In 1905 she led an expedition to the Old Bedford Level to prove it, once and for all.

The Old Bedford Level is very straight as well as very level, and ideal for Lady Blount's purpose. The locals were treated to the sight of this enterprising lady and her friends dangling a large white sheet over the side of a bridge, with the bottom of it just above the water. At Welney bridge, six miles along the channel, one of the earliest telescopic cameras was placed just above water level also, and pointed at the sheet. Now if the earth was round, Lady Blount argued, the bottom of the sheet should be below the line of sight of the photographer at that distance. She was not at all surprised, but understandably delighted, when the photographs showed not only the entire sheet, but its reflection in the water below it.

That was enough for Lady Blount. She would not accept any arguments about the refraction of light over water, or any other explanation. She died in 1923, still utterly convinced that she had made her point. On a misty night along the Old Bedford Level, I am sure you can hear her distant chuckle...

Much later, another remarkable character popped up in that same corner of Norfolk, whose chuckle can be heard, not only among the willows between Downham Market and Brandon Creek, but wherever two or three conservationists are gathered together. David Bellamy was drawn here to applaud yet another new use for the Fens, though basically it is a very old use indeed. After hundreds of years, willows were being cultivated again on a large-scale commercial basis. But this time they would supply the new needs of the twentieth century, which the Fenmen of Popham's time could never have visualised. They were to make willow mats to protect the coast from erosion, and willow fences to protect people alongside motorways from the continuous roar of the traffic. A third of a million willow shoots were planted and besides providing a profitable harvest they also re-created a traditional Fenland habitat for wildlife, which is what brought Mr Bellamy along.

I am sorry he was too late to meet Lady Blount. I can visualise them so clearly together, expounding their views simultaneously as they stroll side by side along the Old Bedford Level, until – if Lady Blount really did get it right – they eventually, fall off the end…

The blank space on the map

Stanford's unspoilt paradise – when the guns stop firing

HERE, AS THEY SAY, IS your starter for ten: Which is the largest Site of Special Scientific Interest (SSSI) in single ownership in England? Here is a clue: if you pick the wrong time and the wrong spot, it is also the most dangerous...

Having now seen it for myself, I can add that it is a most astonishing blend of the beautiful, the battered, and the bizarre. It is of course, the forty-five square miles of Norfolk that used to contain six villages and several farms, and was home for several hundred people. On maps these days it is often shown as a blank. In 1942 the villagers were given three weeks' notice to move out, and it became what is now known officially as Stanford Army Field Training Centre, but is still referred to by most Norfolk people as the Stanford Battle Area.

It seems an unlikely site to be of special scientific interest. Big guns blast away at it, and troops crawl about on it with live ammunition being fired over their heads. For the flora and fauna, that's the bad news. The good news is that for over half a century the land has seen no chemicals, no artificial fertilisers, no intensive farming and no speculative developers. The firing only takes place in particular areas at particular times, so that even the rabbits seem to know when to duck. Much of the Battle Area is inhabited only by wildlife, and kept neatly in trim by thousands of munching sheep.

The Army is proud of its conservation role, and in the lulls between the firing practices and the mock battles it takes authorised parties on a sort of magical mystery coach tour. I was in one of those parties and with me were conservationists, naturalists, botanists and arch-aeologists, all with their special interests, but what fascinated me on the tour was the strange contrasts it offered, like touring a series of deserted film sets.

That is not too far from the truth. A battle area can not only be an SSSI but an SSIF – A Site of Special Interest to Film-makers. There are no interruptions from members of the public, temporary buildings can be put up and taken down without any planning problems, there are no anachronistic telephone wires or TV aerials to be kept out of shot – and so long as they pick a time when the guns are not firing, there are no extraneous noises.

Much of 'Dad's Army' was filmed there, and I saw the Bailey Bridge which Captain Mainwaring and his gallant team defended in one of the episodes. More disconcertingly, we came upon a cluster of genuine log cabins, used by the settlers in the film 'Revolution'; it was a disaster at the box-office, and the director never came back to take them down.

But there are bigger and more sobering surprises than that. We rounded a bend and suddenly we were in Northern Ireland confronted by a replica of an Army strongpoint. Round the next corner, on some rising ground which is the nearest that Stanford can offer to a German hillside, is what looks like a genuine Bavarian village, until you get closer and see that it is mostly breezeblock and corrugated iron. As we drove through it, negotiating the realistic heaps of bomb-damage on the road, I could not read the name on the 'church' noticeboard, but I think the next line was clear enough: 'Patron Saint of Pillaging'...

My biggest surprise, though, was not what I saw but what I didn't see. I fully expected a Somme-like landscape from the First World War, pitted with craters, devoid of vegetation except for the odd blackened tree-stump. But modern shells, I was told, don't make big craters any more; they are designed to explode in the air, to kill more people – and anyway, the firing areas are out of bounds. So the only evidence I saw of recent damage was a distant row of conifers that had been shattered by machine-gun fire.

There was plenty of evidence, however, of earlier destruction. We drove through what was once West Tofts, where only the church now stands complete. Grass mounds and rubble mark the sites of the village school and pub; the shell of the pub survived until 1986, when a bivouacking soldier decided to liven up his fire with a can of petrol...

At Stanford itself there are the shells of six council houses, built in 1938, evacuated only four years later. The octagonal church tower is dwarfed by a new gunnery observation tower.

At Buckenham Tofts only the carriage block survives of the old Hall, and there is no sign of the cricket ground where Douglas Jardine once played. The artificial lake, dug by navvies early this century to enhance the landscaping of Humphrey Repton, now has ropes strung across it for 'watermanship training'. And at the original Tottington the shop where schoolchildren bought sweets on their way home has given place to another reconstructed checkpoint. When the villagers were ordered out in 1942, they were assured that they would return after the war. They never did, of course, and unless it is to be buried in a family grave, I doubt they ever will. With the withdrawal from overseas training areas, and increasing use by other countries, the number of troops using the Battle Area is actually going up every year.

It is perhaps some consolation that the Army is proving a conscientious custodian. Where an avenue of cedars of Lebanon was decimated by gales, for instance, new cedars have been planted. Copses of beech and chestnut are flourishing, lanes are lined by massive oaks, colourful areas of gorse and heather are reminders of the old, untamed Breckland, sweeping expanses of parkland and pasture survive from a more elegant era. The birds and the rabbits – and of course the sheep – are everywhere.

This is by no means just a blank space on the map of Norfolk. Much of it seems more like an unspoilt paradise – until the guns start firing, and another patrol emerges from the ruins of somebody's former home…

Why twitchers love Titchwell

Godwits, marsh harriers, even the odd flamingo

I CANNOT BE THE FIRST person to suggest that Titchwell should be re-named 'Twitchwell'. In medieval times pilgrims made their way to the ancient cross outside the little round towered church, on their way to the shrine at Walsingham. Today about 130,000 birdwatchers a year make a different kind of pilgrimage to the RSPB sign further along the coast road which marks the turn-off to Titchwell Marsh Nature Reserve. It has in fact become the Society's most popular reserve in the country, and its development from little more than a tidal bog is one of Norfolk's most remarkable success stories.

Titchwell was rather overshadowed a year or two ago by the discovery at nearby Holme of the 'Sea Henge', the mysterious circle of wooden posts round an anvil shaped tree trunk about four thousand years old. Speculation about its original purpose ranged from a pagan sacred site to a Bronze Age beach hut, and in spite of appeals to stay away, the sightseers poured in, plus a few emotional druids.

But Titchwell does not need a sea henge to attract the crowds. It was different during my earlier visits when the administration kept a low profile, there was free parking and admission, and we rarely met more than a handful of people. There did not seem to be a lot of birds either, and our greatest excitement was seeing a flamingo, an unlikely splash of pink among the reed beds. We assumed it came from some zoo, but I gather it is still seen occasionally, and no zoo has yet claimed it.

But the world – and the RSPB – has moved on. These days there is a charge per car for non-members, and the visitors' centre with a servery for drinks and snacks. The reserve has acquired its third hide, there is a new boardwalk in an area of the reserve that few people have seen before, and the birds have got so used to human company that you do not have to lurk in a reed bed to see them – some of them come and feed at your feet.

For local people with long memories, this must seem like a remarkable transformation. Until 1953 this was farmland, reclaimed from the sea in the 18th century. It was used for grazing and growing potatoes, except during the war when the Royal Tank Regiment used it as a firing range. They left behind two old tank hulls, a short stretch of concrete road, and on the site of the present Island Hide a winch-house that operated the pop-up targets.

Titchwell Marsh Nature Reserve: spectacular migration

But in the 1953 floods the sea wall was breached, the sea rushed in, and after 200 years the reclaimed marshland became a marsh again. There was urgent repair work to be done elsewhere along the coast so that is the way Titchwell remained, with dunes and a shingle spit forming with the action of the tides.

The marsh was virtually left to its own devices until a small incident in 1970 brought it back into the public eye – or rather, the birdwatcher's eye. A pair of Montagu's harriers were spotted breeding in the reeds. They were there again in 1971 and 1972, and a year later the RSPB bought the marsh for £53,000. Ironically, the Montagu's harriers did not breed there again; perhaps they felt they had achieved their purpose.

But plenty of other birds did, as the work of restoration and conservation progressed and in 1979 the first bittern was spotted at Titchwell. In the following year the first marsh harriers came to breed there, and they have bred every year since.

In 1984 the first avocets arrived, then along came the bearded tits and black-tailed godwits, the skylarks and the shorelarks, the great flocks of Brent geese and widgeon, even barn owls and a rare stilt which is such a familiar visitor the locals call it Sammy. There is also, of course, the odd flamingo…

The sea took a hand again in 1991 when it breached the dunes by the Tern Hide and the area behind them became tidal. More recently in 1996 the last of those dunes were washed away, but by then Titchwell was firmly established in the front rank of bird reserves.

Most of the visitors, of course, are serious twitchers, but I have been there to enjoy the walk through the reed beds and the marshes to the vast stretch of empty beach beyond, and to see if my friend the flamingo has decided to come back too.

At one stage on my last visit I thought that Titchwell must have acquired its own sea henge. According to the RSPB leaflet, 'the falling tide reveals a wide expanse of sand and mud, and the remains of an ancient forest, over 6,000 years old.' When I got to the end of the boardwalk that leads to the beach, there ahead of me at the water's edge was a mass of gnarled and blackened wood, great baulks of it heaped up in the shape of a massive cairn.

In some excitement I reported my find to one of the volunteers at the visitors' centre. He gently explained that the wood did not come from a 6,000 year old forest but from an RAF control tower which was used in the 1950s when the area was a firing range for Meteor and Vampire jets. It was demolished – rather untidily – in 1962.

I suppose I must have seen it many times before, but maybe sea henges can over-excite the imagination. I shall stick to flamingo watching in future.

Titchwell Marsh Nature Reserve Hide

The contrast in the crops

Lavender is the loveliest – but then there's sugar beet

I WAS DRIVING BEHIND A beet lorry past Heacham lavender farm when it occurred to me that Norfolk is the principal producer of the loveliest and the unloveliest crops in Britain. There are few sights to match the purple glory of a field of lavender – and at the other end of the scale, there are few sights less enchanting than a lorry load of sugar beet, viewed from behind through a mud-spattered windscreen.

Yet lavender and sugar beet have certain features in common. They are both comparatively new to Norfolk – they have only been introduced on a commercial basis since the start of the century. They both require specialised production methods to turn the original crop into products which look totally different from the way they started out. And they can both be attacked by a killer disease for which there is no cure – rhizomania in sugar beet, shab in lavender.

It was partly due to shab that lavender came to Norfolk as a commercial crop. In the nineteen-twenties it practically wiped out the main lavender farms in the south-east of England, and those which survived the disease succumbed to the developers. The Surrey suburbs of Mitcham, Carshalton and Wallington were once an expanse of delicate purples and lilacs; now the predominant colour is plain brick-red.

That created an opening in the lavender market and Linn Chilvers spotted it. His father was a botanist with a nursery garden and florist shop in the Heacham and Hunstanton area. Linn joined him in the business after spending some time in Florida. Perhaps it was his newly-acquired American know-how, combined with his inherited knowledge of flowers, that led him into commercial lavender growing after his father died. The first field was planted in 1932; today if you placed all the rows of lavender bushes end-to-end they would make a hedge a hundred and twenty miles long.

That of course is a mere speck of the Norfolk landscape compared with its acreage of sugar beet. If you laid all the beet in Norfolk end-to-end it would disappear into the North Sea and come out somewhere near Stavanger. But this too, is not a native product. While lavender was probably brought into Britain by the Romans, sugar beet only arrived in the early part of this century.

The beet industry originated in Germany around the 1750s and I like to think that Germany's most famous composer had a hand in all this. Could he have invented the oven in which beet was heated to produce sugar and named himself after it – Ludwig van Beet'oven?

The Romans did not need such ingenuity to detect the possibilities of the lavender plant, nor to invent a name for it. It had such an obviously pleasing scent that they used it to perfume their famous Roman baths, and as 'lavare' meant 'to wash' and 'lavandum' fit for washing', they decided to plump for 'lavender'. They still called it that when they found another use for it, as a herbal remedy for various ailments, and indeed it has had its medicinal uses ever since.

But there was a chemical breakthrough with lavender which produced as unlikely a benefit to mankind from this little plant as producing succulent sugar crystals from an ugly root. A Frenchman with the euphonious name of Nicephore Niepce discovered in the early nineteenth century that he could fix an image chemically by combining a special type of bitumen with lavender oil; it changed its solubility depending on how much it was exposed to light. This, so the historians say, was how modern photography was born. Nice one, Nicephore…

Actually, lavender is a lot more versatile than sugar beet, which apart from producing sugar is only used for animal feed or to unseat unwary motorcyclists in country lanes. A herbal medicine, a soothing oil, a fragrant perfume, an early photographic aid – and that's just a start. You can dry lavender for flower arrangements, make sachets to keep the linen drawer fresh and even use it to beat sugar beet at its own game. I am assured, for instance, that a trout stuffed with thin slices of lemon and lavender sprigs, or roast lamb with lavender and redcurrants, can be particularly choice.

But of course it is the lavender oil that provides the best returns, and two-thirds of Norfolk lavender ends up in the distillery. That is hardly on the same scale as the sugar refineries at Cantley and Wissington which process hundreds of thousands of tonnes of beet and produces a third of the nation's sugar. A still at the Heacham lavender farm takes just 250 kilograms of lavender which produces about half a litre of oil; it's not exactly mass production, but it's enough.

It's a very simple process, so simple that when they are filling a still with lavender a man actually climbs in and treads it down to make sure it all goes in. On this sort of scale it is the most effective method; I wouldn't recommend it in a sugar refinery.

The harvesting of the lavender has become as mechanised as sugar-beeting in the last thirty years. About the same time that automatic beet lifters were replacing the rows of men working their way through the beet fields, topping each beet one by one, an old cultivator frame was being adapted at Heacham to replace the workforce in the lavender fields. It used to take forty cutters with their sickle-shaped knives to cut four acres of lavender in a day; one machine can achieve that quite comfortably today.

Neither lavender nor beet is harvested during the conventional harvest time. All those harvest festivals in September and October are much too late for lavender and much too early for beet. The lavender is cut during five or six weeks in midsummer, whereas the beet is still around in January, great piles of it in the fields, lorry loads of it on the roads and the powerful smell of it around the refineries.

But even 'In the beet mid-winter, when frosty wind makes moan,' we can look forward to a more fragrant and delicate harvest in the warmer days to come, under skies that should be lavender-blue.

West Dereham's coprolite

Before modern fertilisers it was the dung thing

JUNE, I AM TOLD, USED to be marling time, the season when marl was dug out of the pits which can still be found all over Norfolk, and spread on the land as a natural fertiliser. These days the pits just contain water, a few trees and the occasional abandoned cooker, but the marl that came out of them was so useful that one early agricultural writer called it 'the great foundation of Norfolk farmers' wealth'.

However, there was another natural feature of the Norfolk soil which could have been just as valuable, yet its name is rarely heard outside academic circles, and even when the name is mentioned, few people know the bizarre origins of this unlikely material.

I first heard about it in West Dereham, a scattered village in the far west of the county near Downham Market, which has little in common with its East counterpart except its name. Its main claim to fame – indeed the only one so far as I know – was the birthplace of Hubert Walter, a versatile 13th century scholar who was Lord Chief Justice, Lord Chancellor, and Archbishop of Canterbury. In his spare time he founded an Abbey at West Dereham where Abbey Farm now stands.

I assumed he would be featured on the village sign, but instead there is a rather humbler figure in a flat cap and smoking a pipe, driving a horse and cart. The cart contains an unprepossessing grey substance that might represent manure – or even marl. But when I made enquiries locally I found it was neither. That stuff, they told me nonchalantly, is coprolite.

I am afraid I was none the wiser. 'What is coprolite?' I asked – and the answer was rather disconcerting. 'Coprolite,' they said, 'is dinosaur dung'…

I like to think I have got used to the vagaries of the Norfolk sense of humour, so I expressed no surprise. 'Indeed,' I said. 'And why is it on your village sign?'

'Because,' they said, without a flicker, 'we used to have a coprolite mine.'

I tried to remain unmoved, but I must have sounded ever so slightly sceptical.

'You mean,' I said, 'you had a mine full of dinosaur dung?'

'That's right,' they said. 'Masses of the stuff.' And detecting perhaps that I might not be entirely convinced, they gently explained. 'It was fossilised dinosaur dung. Most of it went off to a factory in Ipswich, to be made into fertiliser. Good stuff, coprolite!'

'Of course,' I said, and thanked them, but the doubts still lingered. Back home I looked in the dictionary, wondering if it would even be mentioned – and then mentally apologised to my friends in West Dereham. There it was: 'Coprolite: Any of various rounded stone nodules thought to be fossilised faeces of Mesozoic reptiles and animals.' In other words, dinosaur dung.

But there was still another question to answer. Why did all this dung accumulate in one place? Could West Dereham have been some sort of tyrannosaur toilet? The mind began to boggle.

The Norfolk Natural History Unit put me right. The coprolite found at West Dereham, they told me, did not in fact come from dinosaurs. Even more bizarrely, it came from sharks. A couple of hundred million years ago the whole of Norfolk was under the sea. When it eventually emerged as the waters receded, the shark dung was left behind on what was then West Dereham beach. The action of the tides had washed it all into one place, in the same way that today large quantities of shells are washed onto one particular beach.

The source of West Dereham's coprolite

So far, so good. But I cannot help wondering how anyone could guess that these unattractive nodules might be used as a fertiliser.

I suppose the discoverer of coprolite could have been mocked when he first ground it up and spread it over his garden. He might well have just played marbles with it, or even tried to burn it as fuel. But happily he chose the right option, and presumably it worked such wonders on his dahlias that he marketed the stuff – and the idea caught on.

The West Dereham coprolite mine has long since disappeared but the village sign keeps its memory greeny-grey. Coprolite nodules have now become collectors' items, their value depending on what variety of prehistoric creature produced them. It makes me wonder what will become fashionable as collectors' items in the years ahead. I like to think it is encouraging news for those conscientious dog owners – and there are all too few of them – who always carry a little plastic bag to tidy up after their dogs. They could be storing up a valuable legacy for their great-great-great-great-great-grandchildren...

Medieval church treasures

Mermaids on the bench-ends, doom on the walls,
angels in the roof

WHEREVER YOU ARE IN RURAL Norfolk, if you are looking for a permanent art exhibition featuring various combinations of sculpture, wood-carving, painting, metalwork and stained glass, you will not need to look very far. First-rate art galleries exist in nearly every village, and admission is always free. It is not, however, the prime function of these buildings to be galleries; they are places of worship, built to the glory of God.

Norfolk has some 650 medieval country churches, and I have yet to find one which does not contain a worthwhile example of an early artist's work. Mind you, the churches are often works of art in themselves. Many are grand enough to be small cathedrals, erected by wealthy landowners to create their own place in Heaven and outdo their neighbours. But my fascination with Norfolk's churches centres on what I can find inside them – not necessarily great works of art, but works of art that are different from all the others.

Take fonts, for instance. We have some splendid old fonts in Norfolk, beautifully carved by the Normans and their successors. Many of them portray the Seven Sacraments, but I know of only one, at Great Witchingham, which offers a bonus, an eighth panel portraying the Assumption. The Labours of the Month were also considered very font-worthy by stonemasons, and at Burnham Deepdale, for instance, the central character never seems to have a moment's respite from digging, ploughing, sowing, hoeing, reaping, stacking, threshing, digging, ploughing, sowing… The carver at Warham All Saints took a lighter view of the same subject – incorporated in his Labours, for reasons best known to himself, is a hare playing a zither.

All Saints has another delight for the artistically-minded, an alabaster reredos depicting the Last Supper, but I was more taken with a memorial to a former Rector who captained the England Rugby football team in 1900. It intrigued me, not because of his footballing prowess, but because it was erected in his memory by his seven daughters. An England Rugby captain with seven daughters, and no son? Even a man of God must have felt a twinge of frustration...

Angels in the roof at South Creake

Incidentally, the church at the other end of the village, Warham St Mary's, is in the running for my favourite font. As a change from all those heavyweight chunks of four-square Norman stone, the Georgian designer who created this one has left us a slim, elegant receptacle which might be an avant-garde bird-bath.

Early craftsmen lavished as much attention on their font covers as on the fonts themselves. There are several in Norfolk to choose from, but when it comes to the crunch – it's Trunch. The six-legged canopy is like a massive crown on stilts: it must be quite tricky at christenings to manoeuvre the baby between the uprights.

Bench-ends provide an even wider scope for artistic inventiveness. The pews at Wiggenhall St Mary the Virgin, with saints in niches on the ends and traceried carved backs, are said to be the finest in England, though hardly the most comfortable. At a more homely level, subjects range from a mermaid, a woodpecker and a baby in swaddling clothes at Grimston to Thurgarton's howdah-carrying elephant, a very long way from home.

A wall painting at Wickhampton is called 'The Quick and the Dead'. The Quick are three kings hunting deer, the Dead are three skeletons, hunting the kings. Fortunately, most wall paintings are rather less depressing: Shelfanger has the Adoration of the Magi, Weston Longville has a Jesse Tree tracing the ancestry of Christ, while St. Christopher, patron saint of travellers, has done a fair amount of travelling himself around the walls of Norfolk churches, particularly at Hemblington, where the complete story of his martyrdom is portrayed. There are also the unofficial wall decorations, added perhaps while the master mason's back was turned, like the little devil at Beechamwell.

The more conventional artists also turned their talents to stained glass, and there is hardly a church in Norfolk without a creditable example of their work. Norwich had its own school of glass-painting in the 15th century, which produced, for instance, the east window at East Harling, showing scenes from the life of Christ. It includes an unusual view of the Ascension, in which only His feet are shown, just before they disappear into a cloud, while His footprints are left on the ground below.

Painted rood screens are the great speciality of Norfolk churches, and most people know the magnificent ones at Ranworth, Attleborough and Barton Turf, but few people knew about the screen at Wellingham, a tiny parish of 30 people, until the Norfolk Churches Trust chose one of the panels, depicting St George slaying the dragon, for the frontispiece of a Christmas card.

Among the notable examples of other art forms in our country churches I would select the medieval wineglass pulpit at Burnham Norton, Sir Hugh Hastings' memorial brass at Elsing, the brass lectern and chandeliers at Walpole St Peter, the carved roof bosses at Salle, and the winged saints, apostles and prophets poised for take-off up among the roof beams at Knapton. And, of course, there are all those elaborate effigies and marble monuments that have survived, often unscathed, through the centuries. Sadly, many churches are kept locked for fear of damage or theft, and locating the key can be quite an initiative test for genuine visitors. But do visit our village churches, enjoy them, indeed marvel at them – and as you leave remember that offertory box by the door.

Methodist chapels in new guises

'The building has closed, the church remains'

THEY ARE ALMOST AS FAMILIAR a feature of our Norfolk villages as the parish church, and they are held in just as much affection by those who belong to them. But unlike parish churches, which can be very large or very small, very pinnacled and battlemented or very plain, very ancient or very modern, nearly all these buildings were erected in the last century, and from outside they all look very much the same.

Perhaps for this reason they do not attract so many visitors, or feature in so many photographs, or get written about in so many articles – and I am guilty of that myself.

But when a Methodist chapel has to close, there is just as great a sense of loss as when an Anglican church is made redundant. More so in some cases, because the folk who have worked so hard to keep it going probably come from families who have worshipped there since it was built; indeed their grandparents may have helped to build it.

This has happened at Great Dunham, the latest of many. In the 1960s there were 16 chapels on what used to be the Swaffham circuit; with this closure there are just six. The story is probably much the same elsewhere in Norfolk, and the history of Great Dunham chapel must be a fairly typical one.

During the early part of the nineteenth century Methodism was gathering strength in the village, and in 1843 the *Primitive Methodist Magazine* reported that although there had been opposition from a 'religious quarter' it had now been overcome. With its customary eloquence it continued: 'We have obtained a house to preach in, and the word has been like a hammer that breaketh the rock in pieces.

About 30 souls have been converted since we entered the place, and 20 of them joined our Society.'

During the next 20-odd years meetings were held in houses or hired buildings. By 1867 enough money had been raised to build a chapel at a cost of a little over £200. It was to the standard pattern but with a handsome frontage of knapped flints around the arched doorway and the two tall windows. A Sunday School was built on the back about 20 years later.

There are families who have been associated with the chapel ever since, and the name that constantly occurs is Barrett. Arthur Barrett first went to chapel with his parents, his three brothers and his two sisters over 80 years ago. In due course he became a steward, his sister Aggie played the organ, his wife Daisy ran the Sunday School with him until their daughters Jean and Hazel took it over. After the last war this was the only Sunday School in the village until a new Rector arrived and decided to start one at the parish church. Happily the relations between the churches were very different from the 1840s; the Rector and the Barretts worked amicably alongside each other. Indeed, in spite of that early opposition from a 'religious quarter', Anglicans and Methodists co-operated in great harmony.

The Rector took services at the chapel, the Pastor preached in the church. They shared the same organist, Joan Smith, who was taken to the chapel by her grandmother in 1926 and started playing the organ when she was twelve. And John Dawson has been not only a devoted chapel worker but also a member of the parochial church council at St Andrew's.

John showed me around the chapel soon after it closed. Some of the old pews had already been removed and the pulpit was due to go at any time. It is not like a Church of England pulpit, more like a very large child's playpen with elegant balustrades on three sides.

The Methodist chapel at Great Dunham

I gather the balustrades had to be quite sturdy. Ruth Baines, one of the Sunday School pupils who later became a local preacher, remembers sitting beside the pulpit with the other children imitating some of the peculiarities of the visiting speakers. 'Preachers moved about quite a lot in those days, and we often wondered if they would fall out of the pulpit in their exuberance.'

When I saw the pulpit there was no longer that potential hazard. It was down at floor level and its little flight of steps was stored in the schoolroom, behind big folding doors that cut it off from the chapel. When the children gave performances – as they often did – the doors were folded back so the congregation could watch from their pews.

The only reminders left of those days were an old blackboard and easel propped in a corner, with the remains of a text still chalked on the board, and alongside them a wooden shield on a pole which used to be carried by the children, and which said defiantly 'Gt Dunham Methodist Sunday School.'

It was a depressing sight for John Dawson, but he and the chapel steward Jean Gower, whom he assisted for many years, both accepted that the closure was inevitable.

Numbers at services had dwindled and they had no way of raising enough money for their payments to the Circuit and the maintenance of the building. So the little chapel that had seen so many conversions of another kind over the years, was due to be converted itself.

But it will not be forgotten. A number of those who worshipped in it have recorded their memories. The final entry was contributed by the Methodist minister for Dunham, the Rev. Pam Bayliss, and she made this comment: 'To those loyal few who have remained so faithful and worked so hard to maintain the chapel, this is a bereavement. But although the church building has closed, the church remains, for the church is essentially the people. The fellowship will continue and the seeds sown here will grow in other places.'

For every closed chapel in Norfolk and indeed for every redundant parish church, that would be a fitting epitaph.

Delving into dovecotes

Where doves were doves – until they became pigeon pie

NORFOLKMEN ARE NOT TOO SENTIMENTAL about pigeons; they much prefer to shoot them. So if the Norfolk Dovecote Trust had called itself the Norfolk Pigeon-house Trust, which would have been just as accurate, it might have had problems. Even so, the names have been so interchangeable for centuries that it is difficult for most of us to appreciate the difference between a pigeon and a dove.

As I understand it, the doves are the good guys, the pretty friendly ones that make soothing noises and fly about bearing olive branches, while pigeons are the bad guys, the bloated belligerent ones that eat the crops and make a filthy mess. It was actually the good guys who lived in the dovecotes and which people used to eat, a species with an affinity to man, and urban relatives in Trafalgar Square. The wood-pigeons that do all the damage are quite a different lot, which prefer to roost away from man and wouldn't give a thank you for one of those nesting boxes.

The next problem for the Trust, I suppose, was the fact that dovecotes were once a symbol of feudalism; the birds' main activity was to rob the poor of their crops in order to feed the rich with fresh meat. If an exasperated peasant happened to kill one, he could be fined or imprisoned; if he did it again, he could be hanged. Norfolk, always strong on feudalism, was ahead of the field – in fact, in 1549 the number of dovecotes was increasing at such a rate that it was one cause of Kett's famous rebellion. His followers demolished a new dovecote at Sprowston and demanded a halt to further dovecote development – just as many of us are asking today, except he meant pigeons, we mean people.

It didn't seem to do much good. There are many dovecotes in Norfolk that were built long after 1549, right into the last century. In later years the pigeons were kept for shooting rather than eating, but that died out at the turn of the century and the dovecotes, left empty ever since, have now become an endangered species. Hence the Norfolk Dovecote Trust, the brainchild of Mrs Christine Carter of Bale, who formed it after she noticed that a handsome dovecote in neighbouring Thursford was in a bad way. In the next three years the Trust helped its owners to restore it; then it restored one at Bayfield in the Glaven valley, and that was followed by the dovecote at Thornage which was given by Lord Hastings to the Camphill Village.

In the world of dovecote buffs, Norfolk doesn't rate very high. A definitive book by Peter and Jean Hansell makes only half a dozen references to Norfolk and its 'duffus', as they reckon a dove-house is called here, though I've never heard anyone actually say it. Only two of those they list are still in existence, one at Felbrigg Hall under the care of the National Trust, the other at Rougham Hall which has been under the care of the North family since it was built in 1698.

Another two they mention are not dovecotes at all, although the Hansells say that this continues to be 'a persistent claim' among the locals. They are the Slipper House and the Hermit's House at Bawburgh, both dating back to the pilgrimages to St Walstan's Well. The Slipper House did have a row of flight-holes, but the Hansells say this was probably a later change of use 'and perhaps the source of the popular myth'.

Now I would normally take the word of such experts as gospel – until I read John McCann's 'Historical Enquiry into the Design and Use of Dovecotes' published by the Ancient Monuments Society. Not exactly a gripper of a title, but there is some fascinating stuff in it, not least a few gentle knocks at the Hansells. For instance he picks them up for crediting 'Turnip' Townshend of Raynham with introducing the use of turnips as winter fodder – something which I and many others have always loyally believed. Rubbish, says Mr McCann, in suitable academic terms. 'Suffolk yeoman farmers were already growing turnips on a substantial scale as winter fodder by 1660; the practice was extended to Norfolk by 1674. Townshend did not begin farming until 1730…' Oh well, at least Norfolk was well to the fore.

Winter fodder meant fresh meat all the year round, and the gentry no longer had to rely on pigeon pie during the winter – or so I had always thought, and the Hansells obviously thought the same. Again, rubbish, says Mr McCann, and produces pages of evidence to prove that, not only could the gentry eat winter meat in the form of pigs, venison, veal and chicken, but pigeons didn't breed during the winter anyway, so the supply of young squabs dried up during November and didn't start again until about Easter. Among others, he quotes the kitchen accounts of Sir Hamon Le Strange of Hunstanton; between October 1328 and February 1329 pigeons were not mentioned after the first week in November. Yes, but maybe they just got fed up with pigeon pie. I remain confused…

Thank goodness the experts do agree on one point; they commend the dovecote at Rougham and it becomes apparent that Norfolk did in fact produce one of the greatest experts on dovecotes of the seventeenth century. Roger North virtually wrote a do-it-yourself manual on how to build a dovecote, from the size of the doorway – he favoured 4.5 feet high, big enough to get through but not so big that it took up valuable nesting space – to the size and position of the louvres on the roof.

But here again the irrepressible Mr McCann goes into battle. The name used by the *cognoscenti* for these gaps where the birds enter the dovecote is 'glover'; indeed, in order to impress people I have used it myself. But you'll guess what Mr McCann says: rubbish! 'Glover seems to be an obsolete north of England dialect version of louvre.' A glover, he says, is someone who makes gloves.

So what can we believe, if even the experts can't agree? Just the evidence of our own eyes, I think, and that evidence is that Norfolk has a great many more dovecotes than those they mention. For instance, I have been inside the round one at Elmham Park, a splendid little structure with about 400 nesting boxes and amazingly solid walls – the bricks are laid end-on – and the crest of the Sondes family and the date 1840 over the door. There must be many more, and one aim of the Norfolk Dovecote Trust is to list them all for posterity, as well as preserving the better ones. If it succeeds it could be, as it were, its greatest coo!

Chapter two

**Remarkable Norfolk people: Prizefighters,
bodysnatchers and inventors…**

The Baronet and the bodysnatchers

Sir Astley Cooper collected fat fees, many honours
– and quite a few cadavers

NORFOLK HAS PRODUCED MANY NOTABLE doctors and surgeons over
the years, but few could have had such a bizarre background as the
parson's son who died 160 years ago, in February 1841. He was the
most distinguished and certainly the highest-paid surgeon of his time,
a practitioner and lecturer of international repute, held in high esteem
at Court and honoured with a baronetcy. But in the course of his
profession he became involved with all manner of unsavoury
characters in a macabre trade that prospered, with his active support,
during the first 30 years of the nineteenth century.

Eventually there was such a public outcry that the House of Commons
appointed a Select Committee to investigate, and they put a stop to
the nefarious activities of the Resurrectionists, the euphemistic name
for the bodysnatchers who robbed graves to sell the corpses for medical
dissection. One of the Resurrectionists' principal customers and a key
witness at the enquiry, was Sir Astley Paston Cooper, Professor of
Comparative Anatomy to the Royal College of Surgeons, originally
of Brooke in South Norfolk.

Now and again you will come across a grave in a Norfolk country
churchyard that is covered by some sort of iron cage. I used to think
they were put there just to fend off grazing sheep; these days their
only function is to buckle the blades of lawnmowers. But of course
they served a very different purpose, to protect the deceased's remains
from the bodysnatchers.

The practice was particularly rife in areas within range of anatomy
lecturers. Here in Norfolk, happily, the problem was not so great. The

Norfolk and Norwich was not primarily a teaching hospital and in those early days its main speciality was removing stones from bladders, using rum and opium as an anaesthetic. The patients finished up, one might say, completely stoned…

Anyway, there was no need for caged graves in the little churchyard at Brooke when Astley Cooper was born at the Vicarage in 1768, of a well-placed family – his mother was a Paston, of Paston Letters fame. They moved to Yarmouth when his father was made Rector and young Astley developed into something of a tearaway. His most spectacular exploit was to climb the spire of St Nicholas' Church carrying two of his mother's feather pillows, which he emptied over the bewildered populace below. This was not quite the behaviour expected of the Rector's son, and his father apprenticed him to a local surgeon and apothecary in the hope of sobering him up.

The legendary bodysnatchers

It was an inspired move. Astley had always had an interest in medicine. When a young friend had fallen off a cart and cut an artery in his leg he had displayed an instinctive knowledge of first aid by binding up the lad's thigh with his kerchief to stop the blood flow. His apprenticeship soon took him to London where his uncle was conveniently a surgeon at Guy's and, at the age of only 21, he was appointed a demonstrator at St Thomas's Hospital.

It was the start of a dazzling career. His class increased to 400 students, the largest in London. When he was 24 he went into practice and built up his annual income from five guineas in the first year to a peak of £21,000, easily a record. It is said that one rich patient threw him a cheque for 1,000 guineas in his nightcap after a successful operation. Another patient, who happened to be George IV, threw him a baronetcy.

The royal operation was a comparatively minor one, removing a small tumour from the scalp, but for once the great surgeon was nervous; he had not cut open a king's cranium before. Lord Liverpool, one of the Cabinet ministers waiting outside, observed this and took him by the hand. 'You ought to recollect,' he said helpfully, 'that this operation either makes you or ruins you. Courage, Cooper!' This would have unnerved most doctors, but it did the trick with Astley Cooper – and he became Sir Astley as a result.

Yet throughout this spectacular rise to fame and riches, the former teenage tearaway from Yarmouth was doing surreptitious deals at the back door with the Resurrectionists, to ensure a steady supply of cadavers for his students. It was a regular practice for lecturers to make a down payment of £50 in advance, perhaps to cover the initial investment in picks and shovels, then nine guineas per body on delivery – and Sir Astley Cooper, Bart., was in there bidding with the rest of them.

Giving evidence to the Select Committee he made his position clear, and he was reflecting the views of his profession.

'The law does not prevent us from obtaining the body of an individual if we think proper; for there is no person, let his situation in life be what it may, whom, if I was disposed to dissect, I could not obtain. Nobody is secured by the law; it only adds to the price...'

That may sound a little extreme these days, but it did him no harm at all, even after the law was changed and new controls were introduced. In his declining years he was Surgeon-Sergeant to Queen Victoria, and when he died, he left a substantial fortune. His body was buried, with due ceremony, in the chapel of Guy's Hospital. I trust it remains there, undisturbed...

Genius, manic depressive, or just a wimp?

The poems, problems and peculiar pets of William Cowper

I CONFESS I WAS NEVER greatly excited about the poet, William Cowper in my early days as a reporter in Dereham, even though he was one of the town's most notable historical figures. My knowledge of him was scanty, just enough to know why the Congregational Church in the Market Place was named after him – it is built on the site of his house, with woodwork in the vestry which came from his bedroom – and why he was famous enough to be featured in a stained-glass window in the church. I was not so sure about the window itself; one writer has described it as magnificent, another merely calls it 'unfortunate'. But at least I knew whom it represented.

I also knew I had to call him 'Cooper – or better still, 'Kyewper'.

But somehow I found it difficult to get enthusiastic about the man himself. He seemed to match too closely the popular caricature of a poet: over-sensitive, impractical, slightly out of this world, and eventually, alas, out of his mind. The only line of his that I was familiar with – The cups that cheer but do not inebriate – hardly appealed to an ardent beer-drinker. If I thought about him at all, I thought of him, I am afraid, as something of a wimp.

After nearly 50 years, it is high time that I made amends.

I always assumed that Cowper's link with Norfolk only began when he moved to Dereham from Olney in his declining years, but in fact his mother was a Norfolk woman, a member of the Donne family of Ludham Hall. She gave birth to William in November 1731, and died six years later, the first great sadness of his life and one which never left him. Many years later, looking at her picture, he wrote wistfully:

O that those lips had language!
Life has passed with me but roughly since
I heard thee last...

Roughly indeed. It started when he was packed off to a private school in Luton just after her death. He must have been a bit of a dreamer even then, and no doubt seemed even more wimpish to the young lads in Luton in those days, than he did two centuries later to a young reporter in Dereham. They bullied him unmercifully, and it could well have been the combination of grief over his mother and terror of his schoolmates during those early years that permanently affected his mind.

He had his first period in an asylum in his 20s and from what one reads of 18th century asylums, he could hardly have benefited from the experience. Then he became involved with a religious movement called the Evangelical Revival, which ought to have helped, but in fact it merely increased his depression. They were very strong on eternal punishment and the fires of Hell, and poor William constantly had it on his mind, worrying about the welfare of his soul. As one sympathetic commentator wrote:

'It is a sad thought that this kindest and most gentle and pious of poets could doubt that God would be as kind to him as he himself was kind to all other living things...'

Those living things included hares. William kept three of them as pets, which he had tamed himself. He called them Puss, Tiny and Bess, which would have been fine for a six-year-old, but William was a grown man by now and the sturdy countryfolk who were his neighbours might well have come to the same conclusion as the lads in Luton. But happily William now had his defenders and friends who did their best to protect him from the unpleasantries of the world and coax him out of his fits of melancholy.

In particular there were the Unwins, Morley and Mary, a Huntingdon couple who shared his religious views but did not take life – and the doom-laden after-life – quite so seriously. He formed a great affection for them and they took him under their wing. When they moved to Olney in Buckinghamshire, he went with them.

This was the happiest period of a generally sombre life. One of his friends was the local Rector and together they compiled the Olney Hymns. William wrote over 60 of them, most notably *God Moves In A Mysterious Way* and *Hark My Soul, It Is The Lord*, which live on in most of the hymnals.

The Unwins and their friends realised that writing verses gave William something more cheerful to ponder on than eternal Hellfire, and they often suggested subjects for him to write about. One of his patrons, Lady Austen, told him a popular tale of the day about a worthy old draper who borrowed a horse to go on holiday and had some hilarious experiences – and surprisingly, our dreamy hymn writer seized upon it. He wrote *The Ballad of John Gilpin*, a rollicking comic poem that had the whole of London laughing; it would have made excellent material for a Stanley Holloway recitation.

Unfortunately these lapses into frivolity were rare, and he soon sank back into his customary depression, increased by the death of his friend Morley Unwin. His friendship with Mary continued and they became engaged with hopes of starting afresh together in Dereham. But again his depression overwhelmed him, his mind often failed, and instead of enjoying a happy married life Mary acted as nurse and companion.

Then she too became ill. A succession of strokes disabled her, so both of them had to be cared for. In William's lucid periods, when he could appreciate her condition, it only depressed him more. But her devotion never faltered, and when she died she was buried secretly at midnight, in order, so it is said, not to upset him further. During that desperately unhappy period, he wrote some tender lines dedicated to her that I think are his most memorable. Lord Tennyson went further; they were too moving, he said, to be read aloud. Anyone who has watched a loved one dying will know what he means.

Thy spirits have a fainter flow,
I see thee daily weaker grow;
Twas my distress that brought thee low,
My Mary.

Thy silver locks, once auburn bright,
Are still more lovely in my sight
Than golden beams of orient light,
My Mary.

William Cowper died in April 1800. Like his beloved Mary, he too was buried at midnight, a sombre end to a sad story.

A wimp – or a genius? I only know that I wish I could write like that…

The man behind the name on Erpingham Church

Soldier-statesman, benefactor – and bird-lover?

THE LITTLE NORTH NORFOLK VILLAGE of Erpingham might well claim to have the oldest, the highest and most impressive village sign in the county. Is there anywhere else which has had its name displayed in elegant stonework around the top of the church tower for over 500 years?

Admittedly, after all these centuries the name is not that easy to make out. It is further complicated by a decorative 'M', denoting the church's patron saint, inserted between each letter. The name also completely encircles the tower, with only two or three of its letters on each side, so you have to study all four sides – and deduct the surplus 'M's – before you can work out what it is.

Nevertheless, it is good to know that the name has been preserved in such prominence for so long. Even when the tower was struck by lightning in 1721, and one of the pinnacles fell through the roof and smashed the ancient font, the lettering was unharmed. The village too has survived, though its distance from the church suggests it may have uprooted itself at some stage, perhaps because of the plague. But the Erpinghams themselves, the family that took its name from the village and set it in stone on the tower, have long since disappeared.

I find this very sad. Not only is it a loss to the limerick-writers, who would have great fun with a name like that – imagine the baby-sitting Erpinghams who stopped the babies' indigestion by burping 'em – but also these days it seems that only the historians remember they ever existed, even though one of the Erpinghams was arguably the most notable soldier-statesman that Norfolk had ever produced. It takes a fair amount of clout – often literally in those days – to become

Marshal of England, Steward of the King's Household, Constable of Dover Castle, Warden of the Cinque Ports, Privy Counsellor, Knight of the Garter, and at one stage Ambassador to France, though he also enjoyed knocking the daylights out of the French.

Not least, Sir Thomas Erpingham was a great benefactor of Norwich Cathedral – how many millions of worshippers and visitors have passed through the Erpingham Gate since he had it built to mark the victory at Agincourt? Much more recently, as part of the cathedral's 900th anniversary celebrations, a banner bearing his coat of arms was installed over his tomb. But even in his native county, all that most children learn about him at school is from Shakespeare's 'Henry V'.

You remember the meeting between King Henry and Sir Thomas on the night before Agincourt? 'Good morrow, old Sir Thomas Erpingham,' says the King. 'A good soft pillow for that good white head were better than a churlish turf of France.' The old chap answers gamely: 'Not so, my liege. This lodging likes me better, since I may say, 'Now lie I like a King'.' After a few more noble observations, Henry bids him farewell, suitably impressed 'God-a-mercy, old heart, thou speakest cheerfully.'

As it turned out, the doughty old Norfolkman had good reason to be cheerful. As Marshal of Henry's army and Commander of the archers, he played a key role in the victory. Indeed it was he who started the proceedings by throwing his baton in the air and crying 'Nestroque!' Shakespeare seems to have missed that, but presumably it meant, 'Now strike!' – and they did.

Agincourt was merely the culmination for Sir Thomas of a lifetime's service to the House of Lancaster. He fought alongside Henry's grandfather, John of Gaunt, in Scotland and Castile. He accompanied John of Gaunt's son Henry, Earl of Derby, during his exile abroad, returned with him when Richard II was deposed and helped to crown him Henry IV.

Having backed the winning side, small wonder that he accumulated titles and property (including at one stage Blickling Hall) and was able to become a major benefactor in his old age.

The arms on his banner in the Cathedral can also be seen on the Erpingham Gate and in St Andrew's Hall, which he provided as a church for the Black Friars. But in case you have missed them, I can tell you that they are vert, with an orle of martlets and an escutcheon argent.

None the wiser? Nor was I. But I am told that vert, as you might expect, means green, an escutcheon argent is a white shield, an orle is a narrow band around it, and the eight martlets are little birds.

No one, however, could tell me why Sir Thomas was so interested in martlets that he included, one might say, such a rich orle of them on his arms. Were they symbolic of his eight high offices? (He was King's Chamberlain as well as the seven I quoted). Did he win eight great victories – six during the Scottish and Spanish campaigns as well as Harfleur and Agincourt? Or was he just an amateur ornithologist with a sense of humour?

I have my own theory. I like to think he put them there as a parting puzzle for the limerick-writers:

> *'Who can tell what they meant to old Erpingham?*
> *If only the birds had a chirp in 'em...'*

Anna's mum had best-sellers too

Mrs Sewell's stories used to outsell her daughter's

ANNA SEWELL, AUTHOR OF 'BLACK BEAUTY', is one of Norfolk's most famous, if least prolific writers, but it the matronly figure in the shadows behind her whom I find more fascinating, because for years her books outsold *Black Beauty* by the hundred thousand. Since then she has faded into obscurity and today few people have even heard of her books, let alone read them.

Like Inspector Morse, she was known only by her surname. In his case we eventually learned he was christened, rather bizarrely, Endeavour. She could have been christened Virtue because she epitomised the virtuous Victorian matriarch, with unswerving Christian morals and a firm hand to enforce them. She was Mrs Sewell, to whom Anna dedicated *Black Beauty*: 'To my dear and honoured mother, whose life, no less than her pen, has been devoted to the welfare of others.'

That is not the only reference to her in my copy of the book, inherited from my own mother many years ago. This edition, published in 1901, was already the 57th, and sales were on their way to the eventual staggering total of thirty million. The publishers were based in Warwick Lane, London, but their name is very familiar in Norfolk: Jarrold and Sons. If only Jarrolds' current authors could match that figure…

At the front of the book they listed 'The Black Beauty Series of Popular Books' from *The Morals and Emotions of a Doll: A story for Girls*, to *Geordie, The Black Prince* – a story, I assume for Newcastle boys. Also, rather unexpectedly, *Love Unfeigned, or Let Love Be Without Dissimulation*, presumably for adults only. But it was another title that caught my eye: *Patience Hart's First Experience in Service* – by Mrs Sewell.

I had come across her name before while looking up Anna's background, but information about her was sparse. She came from a farming family at Buxton but her father became a ship owner in Great Yarmouth. She was educated at home, brought up as a Quaker, became a governess, then married and had a family. Two years after Anna's birth they moved to London, where she must have noted the poverty around her. In much later years, when she started writing moral tales for children in prose and verse, many were based on the plight of the street waifs of the City.

It is only at this stage, when she is in her sixties, that the reference books start mentioning her. 'Encouraged by her friends,' says one of them, 'she began to write for publication, and one of her stories, *Mother's Last Words*' – and this is where I blinked – 'sold over a million copies.'

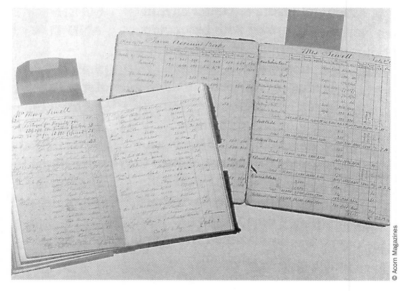

Mrs Sewell's books

A contemporary reviewer wrote: 'This charming poem of two little crossing sweepers has touched the hearts of millions of people.' Another commented: 'Her little tales must have influenced a myriad of lives…'

I was impressed – but puzzled. Over a million copies? Touched the hearts of millions? Influenced a myriad of lives? Then why isn't Mrs Sewell's name as familiar as other great children's writers, J.M. Barrie and the like? Why don't we even know her initials, let alone her first name? Could those reviewers have been just a little over the top?

So I consulted the sober pages of the *Encyclopaedia Britannica*. Mrs Sewell did not rate a separate entry, but she did get a mention in her daughter's as 'a deeply religious popular author of juvenile best-sellers.' However, the term 'best-seller' can cover considerably less than a multitude of sales, and I was still not quite convinced – until I turned to the back pages of my 1901 *Black Beauty*.

Jarrold & Son were not bashful about promoting their wares in their own books, and they filled 35 pages with advertisements for their publications. Most were aimed at children and all were exceedingly worthy. I turned a page and there was Mrs Sewell staring out at me, her engraved portrait filling most of the space, stern-eyed, tight-lipped, a jaw like the prow of a battleship. Her lace bonnet did nothing to soften the formidable features. Here indeed was Victoriana personified.

There was not much room left for words but few were needed. 'Mrs Sewell's Poems and Ballads, Complete in One Volume' was the heading, with the price, three and sixpence. A couple of brief Press commendations and finally, almost casually, in very small print: 'Over 2,000,000 of these poems and ballads have been sold'.

Over two million! At that time, according to another back page, daughter Anna had only notched up her 250th thousand. So there was no doubt about it: in 1901 Jarrolds' star author was not Anna Sewell, but Anna's Mum.

Yet while other Jarrold authors were given their full names, she was just Mrs Sewell. Her portrait seemed to be eyeing me coldly: 'Two million copies, and you don't even know my first name...'

I went back to the reference books, without result. I found 78 Sewell's in the Norwich telephone directory, but I baulked at asking 78 total strangers if they knew the Christian name of Anna Sewell's mother – though a Mr Sewell of Sewell Road, Buxton might have been a likely bet.

But there was another solution. Mrs Sewell outlived her famous daughter by six years, and they buried her in the same graveyard at Lamas, near the family's Buxton home. If it had been the churchyard I could have asked the Rector, but the Sewell's were Quakers, and the Quaker graveyard was no longer in use. So I went to Lamas to look for myself.

The Friends Meeting House had a 'For Sale' notice outside. It also had on the wall facing the road the memorial stones I was looking for. It was one of those rare occasions when research did not even involve getting out of the car. It also meant that anyone in Lamas could probably have told me Mrs Sewell's Christian name without my going there at all.

It was not, as I had half expected, Virtue. The remarkable old lady who died at Catton on June 10th 1884, aged 87 years, daughter of Mr and Mrs John Wright of Buxton and wife of Isaac Sewell, was christened simply, Mary.

Not exactly the literary discovery of the year, but I hope Inspector Morse would approve of my Endeavour.

World champion – in the 44th round!

Why not 'Welcome to Jem Mace's county, it'll knock you out'?

THE IDEA OF MARKETING NORFOLK as 'Nelson's County' had a rather mixed reception, so here is another suggestion for the pundits to toy with. Instead of commemorating our fighting hero of Trafalgar, how about naming the county after our other great fighter, the hero of 500 boxing bouts, who became heavyweight champion of the world? The experts have called him the father of scientific boxing, and his 35 years in the professional ring – the same period that Nelson served in the Navy, but 85 years later – earned him a place in the *Guinness Book of Records*. So how about: 'Jem Mace's County – It Will Knock You Out!'

He was known as the Swaffham Gypsy – no doubt the marketing pundits thought of that one too. But it will only confuse you, because he was not born in Swaffham and he was certainly not a gypsy. He was actually born in 1831 at Beeston, six miles from Swaffham, and he was the son of the village blacksmith, which perhaps accounts for his muscle power. As a lad he joined in the bare knuckle fighting on the village green and by the time he was 14 he had been in a hundred-odd fights – and was winning them all.

Mr Mace senior was not too impressed and apprenticed his son to a cabinetmaker in Wells, perhaps hoping he would develop more artistic tastes – and in a way he did. Jem acquired an old violin from a sailor on the quayside, learned how to play it and wandered off around Norfolk, playing outside pubs for coppers.

In 1849, when he was 18, the story goes that he was playing outside a pub in Yarmouth when three sailors accosted him. One of them was unwise enough to smash his violin. Jem took only five minutes to knock him unconscious, then flattened one of his friends while the other ran away. Admiring spectators had a whip-round so he could buy another fiddle, but one of the more discerning ones told him, 'You've got pluck and a punch in those maulies like a kick of a horse. You should be a prize-fighter, not a fiddler.'

JEM MACE, CHAMPION OF ENGLAND, IN FIGHTING COSTUME.
(From a Photograph by George Newbold, of the Strand.)

Jem Mace, Champion of England and the world!

Jem collected two guineas but he never bought another fiddle. Instead he took that advice and joined a travelling boxing troupe. While he was flattening a succession of opponents in Norwich Market he was spotted by Nat Langham, a former prize-fighter who recognised his potential. He invited Jem to join his own group of fighters for a wage of four pounds a week, plus tuition. He perfected his natural straight left, the counter punch, the jab, all the classics of scientific boxing, but all with bare knuckles.

He had to work for his money. This was not a quick rough-and-tumble with green yokels, it was professional prize-fighting against experienced opponents, with contests lasting two hours or more; they literally fought until they dropped. But thanks to Jem's natural ability and Langham's coaching it was generally the other chap who did the dropping.

But not always. In one fight, Jem's fists became so sore and swollen after thumping his opponent for 50 rounds without knocking him out, that his seconds threw in the towel. Nat Langham was furious, 'I've got no room for weaklings,' he stormed. 'Either you pickle your hands and train yourself into better shape or out you go. No fighter of mine calls it quits after 50 rounds!'

The pickling mixture he prescribed was a potent brew involving copper, gunpowder, whisky and horseradish. If it was too painful to dip your fist in it, I suppose you could always try drinking it. But Jem persevered with the pickling process, until his fists became so hardened it seemed remarkable that he could straighten his fingers, and the towel was never thrown in again.

As his skills and stamina improved, Langham entered him for special bouts and bet heavily on him, with Mace getting his share of the winnings. It was the start of Jem Mace's important successes – and of his fortune.

In due course he fought the English champion, Sam Hurst, humorously nick-named the Stalybridge Infant. The humour was as heavy as the 'Infant'; he weighed 18 stone. Throughout his career Mace was never more than a middleweight, and Hurst looked big enough to eat him.

It took only eight rounds for Mace to knock him out with a straight left between the eyes. He had gained his first championship title at the age of 30. But he was soon challenged by Tom King, a London stevedore built on the same scale as the Stalybridge Infant. This time the fight lasted 44 rounds and it ended with one of Mace's less scientific punches, a looping blow to the back of the neck which would have appalled the Marquess of Queensbury, but in bare-knuckle boxing, anything went.

When King recovered he demanded a return fight and after 22 rounds it was Mace who stayed down. It was such an unexpected result that some accused him of throwing the fight, but in fact he slipped on the blood-soaked grass and fell into the punch.

When King eventually retired Mace claimed the vacant title and went to the States in 1870 to challenge the American champion, Tom Allen. He won in a brief 40 minutes, collected $10,000 and became undisputed world champion.

But for Jem Mace it was rags to riches, then back to rags again. He made more money in America and Australia with boxing exhibitions, and even opened a boxing school in Sydney, teaching Australians how to fight, but he gambled it all away at the Melbourne races and returned to England in the 1880s nearly broke. He kept the Swan in Norwich for a while and still sparred in his mid-sixties, but when the old age pension was introduced in 1900 he was one of the first to apply for it. Ironically, he ended his days as he began; in 1910 he caught pneumonia – playing a fiddle outside a pub.

But let's forget the sad ending and remember the amazing achievement of this village boy from Norfolk, as it is remembered in Beeston churchyard. A marble cross near the gate, 'erected by a few of his old friends', bears the simple inscription: 'Jem Mace – Champion of the World'.

The MP who invented the horsebox

Lord George Bentinck beat the bookies – and has
annoyed other road-users ever since

IN THE GUILDHALL ASSEMBLY ROOM at King's Lynn hangs the full-
length portrait of Lord William George Frederick Cavendish-Bentinck,
remembered in Lynn, if only by a few, as Lord George Bentinck. He
was one of the town's more illustrious MPs, but better known among
racing historians for the remarkable betting coup he pulled off in 1836.
It relied for its success on a new type of vehicle that he introduced on
to the nation's roads and its successors have been serving the
equestrian fraternity – and irritating other road-users – ever since. Lord
George was the inventor of the horsebox.

It seems he shared a talent for devising new modes of transport with
his highly eccentric brother, the fifth Duke of Portland. When the Duke
journeyed to London from the family seat in Nottinghamshire, he used
the 19th century forerunner of the Motorail. His coach was driven
to the local railway station and loaded on to a flat railcar attached to
the rear of the London train. When it got there, a fresh pair of horses
was harnessed up and he was driven to his town house in Cavendish
Square – where else for a Cavendish-Bentinck? He remained inside
the coach throughout the journey.

While Lord George could match his ingenuity in this field – and put
it to a very profitable purpose – he could not equal his eccentricity.
He did have one minor idiosyncrasy regarding his cravats; although
they cost a guinea apiece, he never wore the same one twice. His brother,
however, went in for much more spectacular extravagance. Underneath
the grounds of his home at Welbeck Abbey he created a subterranean
mansion with a ballroom large enough for 2,000 dancers – though

Lord George Bentinck

he never held any dances – a billiard room with 12 full-sized tables, on which nobody ever played, and libraries full of thousands of books, which nobody else ever read. There were 15 miles of tunnels and an underground railway to carry his meals the 150 yards from the kitchen to the dining room.

Lord George was perhaps deterred from similar eccentricities by the effects of his brother's on the family home. The Duke not only turned the grounds into an enormous rabbit warren, he also stripped the house of its treasures, painted most of the rooms pink and installed in each, in full view, a lavatory basin. When Welbeck Abbey was eventually taken over by the Army as a military college, they probably deplored the Duke's taste in interior decoration, but they might have been tempted to reward his talent for tunnelling by making him Colonel-in-Chief of the Royal Engineers.

Lord George, however, preferred to obtain his honours in the more traditional way – using the family connections. The Cavendishes and the Bentincks, and later the Cavendish-Bentincks, had served their country with distinction as politicians and diplomats. Lord George himself started his political career as secretary to his uncle, Lord Canning, who just happened to be Foreign Secretary. Small wonder that he became MP for Lynn when he was still only 26 years old.

Politics, however, was not his first love. He was primarily interested in owning and breeding racehorses – and he did it most successfully. The culmination of his racing career came in 1848, the year of his death, when his horse, Surplice, won both the Derby and the St Leger.

But he carved himself a more unusual niche in racing's Hall of Fame much earlier than that. In 1836 he won the St Leger at Doncaster with a horse that all the bookmakers believed would be a non-runner. It had raced at Goodwood, more than 200 miles away, only three days before and in the normal way racehorses were walked from one course to another, allowing plenty of time for them to rest up once they got there, before the race.

So the Doncaster bookies assumed there was no way a horse from Goodwood could get there in time and they cheerfully offered extremely long odds to anyone who was idiot enough to back Lord George's entry. The astute Lord George, through his agents, made sure that plenty of idiots did...

On September 18th he duly raced his three-year-old thoroughbred Elis at Goodwood, for everyone to see. Then the horse was led away well out of sight of the racecourse and loaded into the prototype horsebox that Lord George had designed. It was a closed van with a padded interior, large enough to take two horses, and drawn by six more. It had been built for him secretly by his London coachbuilders, appropriately named Herring; Lord George was very fond of the red variety.

The horsebox headed north, from Sussex to Yorkshire. It averaged a brisk 75 miles a day and it arrived at Doncaster in time for Elis to step out of it, fresh as a transplanted daisy – and win the St Leger by two lengths. In his excitement Lord George may have forgotten to patent his new invention, but the money it helped to win that day was ample compensation.

So, if you have a chance to visit the Assembly Room in King's Lynn Guildhall, don't miss the portrait of Lord William George Frederick Cavendish-Bentinck. It shows him with his hand resting on some papers and a half smile on his face. The papers are meant to be official ones, but I suspect that they are actually the racing pages of *Sporting Life*. And we all know why he is smiling...

He prosecuted Raleigh and the gunpower plotters

Sir Edward Coke gave them quite a rocket

EACH YEAR WHEN WE remember, remember, the fifth of November, we call the effigy on the bonfire a 'guy', in memory of the man who nearly blew up the Houses of Parliament. So as we set fire to it perhaps we should also call ourselves 'teds', in memory of the Norfolkman who virtually sent him to his death on the scaffold.

The Attorney General who prosecuted Guy Fawkes and the other ringleaders was the formidable Sir Edward Coke, later Lord Chief Justice, born in Mileham, who bought his first ten acres of Norfolk soil for five pounds when he was 26 years old and finished up with the vast Holkham estates.

An inscription in Tittleshall church, where he is buried, describes him as 'one of the most illustrious lawyers of all time, and one of the stoutest defenders of the rights of the people'. He is best remembered perhaps, for coining the phrase 'An Englishman's home is his castle', which became a basic tenet of the law. But the ways of the legal profession in the early 17th Century were not quite as exemplary as they are today, and the trial of the Gunpowder Plotters was hardly Sir Edward's finest hour.

According to the historians, it was not so much a trial as a public relations exercise staged by the Secretary of State, the Earl of Salisbury. If Sir Edward was one of our most illustrious lawyers, Lord Salisbury was one of our most devious politicians.

He briefed the Attorney General to present the plot as an international Papist conspiracy planned by the Jesuits, even though all the evidence showed that only a handful of dissidents were involved, with no support from the Catholic church. He also told Sir Edward to make sure the

King got the personal credit for discovering the plot – whereas the whole affair had been watched from the outset by Salisbury's agents.

Sir Edward's courtroom style was not exactly restrained. There had been a good example of it a couple of years earlier at the trial of another famous defendant accused of treason. 'Thou hast an English face but a Spanish heart, and thyself art a spider of Hell,' roared the sturdy Norfolkman. 'You are the absolutest traitor that ever was, the most vile and execrable traitor that ever lived!' Which perhaps is not everyone's picture of Sir Walter Raleigh…

Raleigh himself kept his cool, 'Your phrases will not prove it, Mr Attorney.'

'Thou viper!' blasted Coke 'There never lived a viler viper on the face of the earth!'

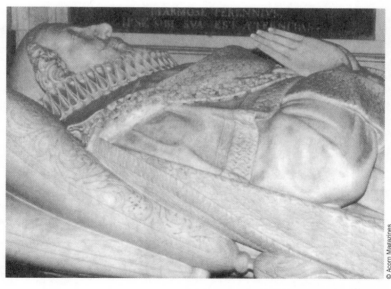

Sir Edward Coke's tomb at Tittleshall Church

Not quite in the Perry Mason class, perhaps, but of course he won the verdict, and Sir Walter found that an Englishman's home could be his Tower as well as his castle.

However, the Attorney General did not need his cross-examination skills for Guy Fawkes. The evidence had already been taken – with the help of the odd thumbscrew – and the verdict was never in doubt. There were no defence lawyers; Sir Edward had the field to himself – and made the most of it. 'This intended crime was such as no man can express it,' he said, but still managed to express it for hours.

Following Lord Salisbury's brief, his fiercest attack was not on the accused but on the Jesuits in general – 'men that use the reverence of religion, yea, even the most sacred and blessed names of Jesus, as a mantle to cover their impiety and treason…'

After exhausting his considerable invective against the Catholics, he followed his second instruction, to credit the King with discovering the plot. 'How the King was divinely illuminated by Almighty God, like an Angel of God, to direct and point as it were to the very place, to cause a search to be made there.' And for good measure he threw in a few extra thoughts about the King – 'his rare and excellent endowments and ornaments both of body and mind, his true and constant religion and piety, his justice, his learning above all kings christened, his acumen, his judgement, his memory…'

Small wonder, you may think, that the King made him Lord Chief Justice. But to be fair, Sir Edward took a far less obsequious attitude after his appointment, and stood up so firmly against the King's blatant efforts to set aside the law that he finished up in the Tower for a time himself. Sir Walter Raleigh, wherever he was by then, must have had a quiet chuckle.

There is one aspect of Sir Edward's link with the Gunpowder Plot that has had a strange sequel in Tittleshall church.

Another defendant, Sir Everard Digby, was tried separately and pleaded to be beheaded instead of suffering a traitor's death, so his wife and family should not lose his estate. He got the full blast of Sir Edward's wrath.

'Oh, how he doth now put on the bowels of nature and compassion; but before, when the public state of his country, the King, the Queen, the tender Princes, were designed to a perpetual destruction, where was then this piety, this religious affection and care?' And he quoted a Psalm at him: 'Let his wife be a widow, and his children vagabonds; let his posterity be destroyed, and in the next generation let his name be quite put out.'

Sir Everard was hanged, drawn and quartered like the rest, and most of his estate was forfeited, but his name was not 'quite put out'. His son became Sir Kenelm Digby, a founder member of the Royal Society, noted author, naval commander and diplomat, and the name of Kenelm Digby has been preserved through all the generations that followed.

Close by Sir Edward Coke's magnificent tomb at Tittleshall, there is a simple wooden cross that was brought from France after the First World War. It is in memory of a Rector who volunteered as a private in the Norfolk Regiment and was killed at Faumont on October 18, 1918, less than a month before the Armistice.

His name was the Rev Lionel Kenelm Digby...

Honoured in America, Canada – and now at home

George Vancouver has a statue at last

FOR A MAN WHO WAS one of England's greatest navigators and surveyors, whose maps were so meticulously accurate they were relied on for more than a century, George Vancouver is remembered very little in his own country and remained largely ignored for two hundred years in the town where he was born. He has been honoured far more in the areas he charted thousands of miles away. Vancouver in Washington State has an impressive memorial to him; Vancouver in British Columbia has a statue of him, and Vancouver Island's capital city of Victoria has him perched loftily on the roof of its government building.

All that King's Lynn had to offer was a small plaque on the site of his home, his portrait in the Town Hall and of course, the Vancouver Centre, an unremarkable pedestrian shopping precinct which Captain Vancouver might well have exercised his navigational skill to avoid…

Enter Bryan Howling, past Mayor and noted Vancouver buff. For years he has been cultivating links with the North American Vancouvers, giving talks and slide shows about his hero and accumulating Vancouver memorabilia from museums and government archives all over the world. His collection ranges from copies of the original charts to a letter from the King of Hawaii to George III asking why he had not received the help that Vancouver had promised. In those days, incidentally, Hawaii was spelt Owhyee – and indeed, Owhyhee not?

It was Bryan's ambition to have a statue erected in King's Lynn for the Millennium to commemorate its most famous seafaring son. It nearly got one in 1936 when the mayor of Vancouver BC, a Mr McGeer, came on an exchange visit and offered to provide it. But in reporting the offer, the local paper added the proviso, 'City of London to Decide', because the Lord Mayor had been much involved. Somehow it never materialised.

My knowledge of Captain Vancouver was as sketchy as most people's and I called on Bryan Howling to get some background. An hour and a half later, after hearing about Vancouver's life and times, looking at his documents, and watching a potted version of his slide show, I almost felt I had sailed on board HMS *Discovery* myself.

Statue of Captain George Vancouver

Here is a flavour of what I learned; first of all, about his name. Vancouver is not exactly common in Norfolk; it originates from Van Couverben in Holland, but not even Bryan Howling knows how the Vancouvers came to be in Lynn. The earliest trace is of George's grandmother Sarah. She must have moved in the right circles because her son John married Bridget Berners from one of the leading local families, and he became Deputy Collector of Port Dues, not just a humble tax collector but an officer of some importance in the town.

The Vancouvers produced six children, three boys and three girls. George was born in 1757 and went to school in a chapel that also served as the town's charnel-house; the boys were taught above, the bones were stored below. When he was 14, perhaps because of his family contacts – the Berners knew the Walpoles, the Walpoles knew Lord Sandwich at the Admiralty – he was able to enter the Royal Navy as a trainee midshipman to sail with Captain Cook on his second marathon voyage.

Young George was away for three years and sailed a distance equivalent to three times round the world. The expedition's main purpose was to find an undiscovered continent north of the Antarctic icefield; in those three years Cook proved conclusively that it wasn't there. Before he finally turned the ship for home, Vancouver climbed out onto the bowsprit at the front, so he could claim he had been further south than any other man on earth.

A year after returning home, George Vancouver again sailed with Cook to look for a northern passage from the Pacific to the Atlantic. They failed and returned to Hawaii for the winter. Trouble broke out with the natives and Cook went ashore to sort it out, accompanied by Vancouver. There was a skirmish, Cook was killed, Vancouver and the rest of the party retreated to the ship. Later there was a reconciliation and the natives brought back Cook's remains – in pieces, so it is said.

They also brought Vancouver's hat which had been knocked off in the fighting.

In the 1790s Vancouver was back in the same area again, this time in command. He mapped the coast from California to Alaska with painstaking thoroughness. No doubt in memory of his Norfolk childhood, his maps included names like Port Snettisham, Port Townshend and the Lynn Canal. It all took him four years and he returned home a sick man. His illness proved fatal and he died soon afterwards in Surrey aged only 40. He was buried in Petersham churchyard in an unobtrusive grave which is maintained by the people of Vancouver BC. Every year on his anniversary, King's Lynn Sea Cadets from the Training ship *Vancouver* lay a wreath on his grave, together with the Agent-General for British Columbia.

Vancouver died before he could finish this three-volume journal of the voyage, so his brother John finished it for him and sent it to the King with a covering note. Well, not so much a covering note as an epistle, 'presuming to hope you will vouchsafe to accept it.' But it did contain a fitting tribute to Captain George Vancouver which Bryan Howling heartily endorses: 'The following pages will prove to Your Majesty that he was not undeserving the honour of the trust placed in him; and that he has fulfilled the object of his commission from Your Majesty with diligence and fidelity.'

Yes, he deserves that statue, which was unveiled by the Duke of Edinburgh in Millennium year. And Bryan Howling might deserve a place on Mastermind – specialist subject, Captain George Vancouver RN of King's Lynn.

The original nosey parker

Matthew was a shrewd operator too

YOU DON'T HAVE TO BE an interfering busybody to be nicknamed 'Nosey'. That is how the Duke of Wellington was referred to by his troops, but only because of what kindlier folk would call his strongly accentuated aquiline features. So was Oliver Cromwell, though his nose was not aquiline, just large and red. But when Nosey is combined with the name of a Norfolk cleric called Matthew Parker, it takes on the more familiar meaning, and it has been associated with him ever since – even though he was Archbishop of Canterbury.

Brewer's Dictionary of Phrase and Fable, that invaluable source of unlikely information, explains why. 'He was noted,' it says, 'for the detailed articles of enquiry concerning ecclesiastical affairs generally and the conduct of the clergy, which he issued for the Visitations of his province and diocese.'

Which sounds pretty stuffy, but hardly seems to merit epitomising him as a 'Nosey Parker'. In a period of religious upheaval in the 16th century, when no one in high office could be sure how long his head would stay on his shoulders, it strikes me as very sensible for an archbishop to keep a close eye on his clerics, in case they turned against him.

So let's bang a drum for the original Nosey Parker, perhaps the most talented and least appreciated of East Anglian archbishops. He assembled a library of Anglo-Saxon manuscripts, which is said to be the finest in the world, and achieved a settlement between religious factions who were just as bitterly opposed as you can find in the Middle East, or Central Africa, or Northern Ireland today. He was also a very shrewd operator, a skill that was virtually essential for an archbishop in the turbulent days of the Tudors.

When he was ordained in 1527 England was still a Catholic country. His first shrewd move was to be a convert in the early stages of the Reformation. After a spell as Rector of St Clement's in Norwich, where he was born and educated, he became dean of a college of priests in Suffolk, not too far from his old friends in Norfolk. They may have included the Boleyns at Blickling or they may have had contacts at Court. However it happened, he became Anne's chaplain during her final days and he was with her just before her execution.

Matthew Parker

The story goes that she placed her three-year-old daughter in his care, which could have presented problems for the dean of a college of priests. But the shrewd fellow realised that the King's daughter, albeit an unwanted one, might be a very useful ally later. He was right. Soon after she became Queen Elizabeth, he became Archbishop of Canterbury.

But that was some years ahead. In the meantime Nosey became master of Corpus Christi, his old Cambridge college, and for a time doubled up as Vice-Chancellor of the University. It was during this period he made his public debut as a mediator, back on his home ground in Norfolk – and it was a spectacular failure.

He was visiting his family in Norwich when Robert Kett and his 20,000 followers set up camp outside the city on Mousehold Heath. They were said to be summarily executing those who had been oppressing them and Parker, quite courageously, decided to try and calm things down. Kett's men did not take kindly to his arrival – was this the first occasion, one wonders, when he was called a Nosey Parker? – and they started menacing him with pikes and arrows.

Parker, shrewd as ever, decided to distract them temporarily by holding a service, which they dutifully attended. It was during the singing of the *Te Deum*, it is said, that he slipped discreetly away…

Back at Corpus Christi he started building up the college library that is still there today. Rare ancient manuscripts were fairly easy to come by after the Reformation, with the monasteries dissolved and their property scattered.

The library's security arrangement was another example of his shrewdness. He decreed that if more than a certain number of books were lost, the rest of them would be handed over in their entirety to another college. Corpus Christi made very sure they weren't.

When the Catholic Queen Mary came to the throne Parker's shrewdness stood him in good stead. He promptly resigned, announced his retirement and kept his head down. Then Elizabeth became queen and her old debt was repaid.

As Archbishop of Canterbury he devised a formula for mollifying the moderates on both sides of the religious divide and isolating the extremists. His rewritten version of the articles of religion became known as the *Thirty-Nine Articles*; they are still printed in the traditional Book of Common Prayer and Church of England priests still have to subscribe to them.

This time Matthew Parker's efforts as a mediator were more successful. Admittedly the more devoted Roman Catholics and the more extreme Protestants never accepted his formula, but at least he established the Church of England as the moderate middle way, and the revised Bishops' Bible which he organised and helped to translate kept most people happy. One might call his achievement, with apologies to a certain well-known open space in the heart of Cambridge, 'Parker's Peace'.

Certainly in any league table of archbishops originating in East Anglia – and there have been quite a few over the centuries – I reckon Nosey Parker wins by rather more than a nose…

Not only the Lincolns and Thomas Paine

A Spelman, a Townshend and Temperance
Flowerdew sailed to America too

THOMAS PAINE, THE THETFORD-BORN radical thinker and writer, has an impressive statue in the town where the Thomas Paine Society assemble each year to mark the anniversary of the man credited with being the inspiration behind the American Revolution, and who coined the phrase, 'The United States of America'. To the colonists he was a hero; to the British government at the time I suspect he was just a Paine.

Thomas is one of the better-known links between Norfolk and the American colonies, along with John Rolfe of Heacham, who brought Princess Pocahontas as his bride, and the Lincolns of Hingham, ancestors of President Abe. But there are many other Norfolk emigrants who played their part, as far back as the *Mayflower* – and beyond.

Even the *Mayflower* itself is claimed to have a Norfolk connection. The little brigantine was registered at Harwich, but the Norfolk writer and historian John Ryden Harris noted that a *Mayflower* was built at Blakeney towards the end of the 16th century when it was a thriving sea-port. In 1588 it was one of the ships that was offered by King's Lynn to serve against the Spanish Armada.

After that it spent most of its time carrying wine imports from Europe to Lynn and by 1620, the year that the Pilgrim Fathers set sail for America, it must have been getting a little weather-beaten, to say the least. But the *Mayflower* that went to America was no spring chicken either; it was described as 'a little, leaky ship'. There does seem a sporting chance that it was the same one.

The Mayflower *sailed to America*

Certainly East Anglia was well represented among the hundred-odd pilgrims on board. But the colony of Virginia was founded some 13 years before the *Mayflower* set sail – and on that occasion Norfolk not only provided many of the emigrants but many of the place names for the colony too, with Norfolk, Virginia at the top of the list.

A number of those early Norfolk colonists made quite a mark. John Pory of Thompson, for example, became the first Secretary of the Council of Virginia, and his cousin, the delightfully-named Temperance Flowerdew from Hethersett, married the Governor of the new colony, Sir George Yardley.

But not all of them fared so well. Ryden Harris tells the story of young Henry Spelman, son of a High Sheriff of Norfolk, who sailed to Virginia in 1608 when he was still a boy and was captured by the Indians.

His life was spared, thanks to the intervention of Princess Pocahontas (later Mrs Rolfe) and Henry spent two years with the Indians learning their language and their customs. After he was eventually rescued he often spoke up on their behalf, making himself very unpopular with the other colonists. On one occasion he was brought before their General Assembly for 'speaking irreverently and maliciously against the present Governor'.

In spite of that, he became the Governor's personal interpreter for five years, but while still a comparatively young man he was one of the casualties in an Indian raid on Jamestown – killed by the very people he had championed.

The Spelmans were squires of Narborough at the time, and I visited Narborough church to see if there was any more information about the hapless Henry. All Saints is full of Spelman monuments and bronzes, which is not entirely surprising. Sir John Spelman, who was given the Narborough estate by Henry VIII for preparing his indictment against

Anne Boleyn, found time from his duties as Justice of the King's Bench to have 20 children.

His descendants included another lawyer, a Recorder of Nottingham whose robed effigy stands on a plinth in the chancel. During restoration work his coffin was found standing on end inside the plinth; apparently he disliked the thought of being trodden upon...

I found the monument to the High Sheriff and his wife on the wall opposite, a very grand affair with the pair of them lolling nonchalantly alongside one another, each resting comfortably on an elbow, and above them a kneeling child and a baby in its cot.

But I also found a problem. The High Sheriff's name according to the story was Harry but on the monument it is Clement. The inscription says he had two sons, but one was also called Clement, the other was John. There is no mention of a Henry.

There were other Spelmans at Congham, including a Henry, but he went down in history as an antiquary, not a High Sheriff, and unfortunately the Spelman chapel at Congham church and their home in Congham Woods have long since disappeared. But another branch of the family used to live at Wickmere, where the round-towered church of St Andrews has some splendid memorials to them.

The good news is that all the male Spelmans were called Henry or Henricus. The bad news is that the earliest memorial is dated 1698, 90 years after the young Henry sailed for Virginia.

Could he have been the son of an earlier Henry Spelman of Wickmere whose memorial has not survived, another High Sheriff of Norfolk about the time Virginia was founded who perhaps took over the office from his kinsman, Sir Clement at Narborough? There are no Spelmans around these days to ask but I like to think so...

While they have faded from the scene, the Townshends of Raynham prospered both here and in Virginia – and ended up on opposite sides. Thomas Townshend emigrated about the same time as Henry Spelman, but managed to avoid the Indians and built a new Raynham Hall on the banks of the River Hudson.

Generations later, when the British Government imposed tax on the colonists, it was a Townshend of Raynham Hall, Virginia, who stretched a massive metal chain across the Hudson to halt British ships; it is still preserved at West Point Military Academy. And the Chancellor who imposed the tax? It was Charles Townshend of Raynham Hall, Norfolk.

So when the Thomas Paine Society remember the Norfolkman who helped to inspire the American War of Independence, perhaps they may also spare a thought for the Norfolkman who helped to provoke it...

Battling women, with sword, pen and guile

From a latter-day Boadicea to a female Pimpernel

A WOMAN'S PLACE, THEY USED to say, is in the home, and in good old feudal Norfolk some folk say it still, albeit under their breath. But Norfolk women have been sallying forth from their homes ever since Boadicea – the best known of the county's battling ladies – led the Iceni rebellion against the Romans.

But she wasn't the only one. In 1421 Margaret Mautby was born at Mautby Hall, a few miles from Yarmouth. The name of Mautby has not been writ very large in the popular histories of Norfolk, but Margaret acquired a much more famous name when she married into the family just up the lane, at Caister Castle. As Margaret Paston she was not only responsible for a great many of the renowned Paston Letters, but she also led the defence of her husband's properties during the stormy years of the Wars of the Roses. While he was away she had to cope with the defence of Caister Castle and the manors at Hellesden and Drayton, but her most spectacular display of fighting spirit was at Gresham Castle. For a time she held out with just 12 servants against a force of 1,000 men, until the attackers mined the walls and set their 'pans of fire' under Margaret's room to smoke her out. Even so, with remarkable devotion and courage, she refused to admit defeat and had to be carried out bodily as the castle fell.

Courage was also the attribute of the more widely recognised Nurse Edith Cavell, but she was not the only Norfolk heroine who carried out a clandestine operation to rescue prisoners from the Continent. Charlotte Atkyns of Ketteringham Hall may not have been very successful, but she did set her sights rather high. During the French Revolution she attempted to rescue Queen Marie Antoinette, and having failed in that, she devoted her energies to rescuing the Queen's little son, the Dauphin.

Charlotte was in fact a female Scarlet Pimpernel. She was an actress at Drury Lane before marrying Edward Atkyns and travelling to France with him in the days before the Revolution. Thanks to his connections she met Marie Antoinette and they became close friends. So when the Queen was imprisoned and sentenced to death Charlotte resolved to rescue her. Disguised in men's clothes she tried to gain admittance to Marie Antoinette's quarters in the Temple Prison in Paris. Her plan went wrong and although Charlotte escaped with her life, Marie Antoinette went to the Guillotine.

Charlotte did not give up. She spent the family fortune on saving the Dauphin and died in poverty in Paris where she was buried in an unknown grave. The only reminder in Norfolk of this brave and determined lady is a plaque in Ketteringham Church.

But two Norwich women – Harriet Martineau and Amelia Opie – have their names preserved in Martineau Lane and Opie Street. Both fought for the anti-slavery movement but they were very different characters and led very different lives. Harriet was born without a sense of smell or taste and was deaf when she was 18. Soon afterwards her father's business collapsed and he died from the shock, then her fiancé died from a brain tumour. Small wonder she was a sad and serious lady who devoted her life to sad and serious subjects. In 1834 she went to America and joined the Abolitionists, and it was the powerful article she wrote in a London magazine on her return that drew the public's attention to the iniquities of the slavery laws in the States.

Amelia on the other hand married a well-known artist and enjoyed herself in London's arty set writing novels and exchanging bons mots. But she too became involved in the slavery issue. She joined the Anti-Slavery Society and represented Norwich at its London convention in 1840. Unlike Harriet, she enjoyed splendid health, and when in her 80s she was at last confined to a wheelchair, she enlivened a visit to the Great Exhibition at the Crystal Palace by challenging another chair-bound old lady to a race around the grounds…

Anti-slavery seems a rather remote cause for Norfolk women to pursue but there was a form of near-slavery here in rural Norfolk, the lives endured by the poorer farm labourers and in particular their wives. Another Norwich woman, Mary Mann, married a Shropham farmer in 1871 and was appalled by the poverty and brutality that existed around her. Through her novels, notably *The Fields of Dulditch*, she swept aside the roses-round-the-door image and exposed the real rigours of rural life.

Another Norfolk novelist, Doreen Rash, better known as Doreen Wallace, campaigned on behalf of the farmers. As president of the National Tithe Payers' Association, and with her husband's support, she refused to pay the Church of England tithe on their farm at Wortham. One year their pigs and cattle were seized, another it was their bedding and furniture, but she lived to see the tax abolished in 1967. When she died, aged 92, she was described as 'a latter-day Boadicea' – which neatly takes us full circle.

Chapter three

Places with strange tales to tell: A bridge, a
garden, an abbey…

The four red hands of Homersfield

A bizarre crest on England's oldest concrete bridge

THE RIVER WAVENEY HAS NEVER presented a major obstacle for anyone intent on entering Norfolk from the south. Close to its source, in Lopham Fen, you can probably clear it with a bound, though not without getting your feet wet. Lopham Fen is a very damp place indeed.

As it flows eastward the Waveney becomes much wider of course, and when it reaches Breydon Water it is very wide indeed, but there are plenty of bridges linking Norfolk with foreign parts. Some of them are delightfully picturesque, like the Nun's Bridge at Thetford, on the route the Romans took, and the series of narrow little bridges across the divided waters at Ellingham Mill. There are also one or two more depressing crossings, like the bridge in Bungay's industrial area. And there are a few very modern ones that are so boring you are hardly aware you are crossing a river at all.

The Waveney has one bridge, however, which can claim a unique place in bridge-building history. It may look like just another nice old bridge, a little the worse for wear, but Homersfield bridge is actually the oldest one in England made of concrete. It is nothing like the anonymous concrete bridges of today – and the new bridge, which replaced it only a hundred yards down-river, provides a good comparison. When the old one was built, concrete was still something of a novelty, and bridges were still being built curved instead of flat.

The man responsible was Sir Robert Shafto Adair, the first and only Lord Waveney. It was built to provide easier access to his home and estate at Flixton Hall, but he closed it one day a year from sunrise to sunset to remind the locals that it was private property. A chain was erected across it and his men charged vehicles for the privilege of crossing it, at the rate of tuppence per wheel. His Lordship always selected a day when the river was in flood, so nobody could dodge payment by driving through the water. Pedestrians were allowed across for nothing if they were nimble enough to negotiate the chain.

Flixton Hall has long since gone, demolished in 1953 when the estate was sold, and so has Lord Waveney and his title, but the bridge was still used by foot traffic and a few years ago it was restored by county councils and preservation societies on both sides of the Waveney. They also restored the crest of the Adair family on the side of it, with its four red hands, a reminder of the strange story that is linked to Lord Waveney and Flixton Hall.

Legend has it that a pantry boy was thrashed to death in his bedroom at the Hall. As he lay dying, he tried to struggle to the door, and his hands left four bloody imprints on the wall. So the Adairs had four red hands incorporated in their coat of arms and a white flag bearing those bloodstained hands flew over the Hall. The Adairs were doomed to bear this stigma for four generations, but one hand could be removed from the crest as each succeeding generation died. However, the title became extinct and the four bloody hands remain on the Homersfield bridge.

So much for the legend, and you can read it in greater detail on the bar of the nearby Swan Inn, where such tales are of course good for business. I have to say though, that the story of a bloody hand crops up in other distinguished families, such as the Holtes of Aston in Birmingham. A stained glass window in their parish church depicts the family crest, which incorporates a red hand minus a finger.

Sir Thomas Holte was rumoured to have killed his cook in 1606, either by running him through with a spit or splitting his head with a cleaver. Either way, it must have made his hands rather red. Sir Thomas took a neighbour to court for repeating this story and won his case, but the rumours persisted, and by the 19th century everyone in Aston was convinced that the red hand in the coat of arms was symbolic of Sir Thomas's crime. The missing finger is explained in the same way as the Homersfield legend – one was removed for each generation and this was the first to go.

I suspect however that these and other 'bloodstained hand' stories are all linked with the armorial Red Hand, which is not confined to Ulster but appears on the coats of arms of English as well as Irish baronets. Sir Robert Adair, like Sir Thomas Holte, was a baronet, though in later years the sixth baronet, Major-General Sir Allan Shafto Adair, had only one son who was killed in action during the Second World War. Members of the family still live at nearby Harleston.

However suspect the legend of the Flixton Hall bloodstains may be, I am all for preserving such stories, just as much as preserving old concrete bridges. What a pity that such a delightful title as Lord Waveney cannot be preserved as well.

Two towers which caused a towering row

Town versus gown – or cassock – at Wymondham Abbey

IT IS NOW MORE THAN 550 years since the monks of Wymondham celebrated the up-grading of their ancient Priory to an Abbey. After being under the jurisdiction of the Abbey of St Alban's, the King granted a petition for its independence in 1448.

But I imagine that meant very little to the man in the Wymondham street. The same monks were installed there, their new Abbot was the former Prior. The locals were probably much more interested in the feud that had been going on for many years between Town and Gown – or Town and Cassock. Certainly the feud makes a much more intriguing story, particularly as the Abbey was dissolved 90 years later by Henry VIII, and its status was lost altogether.

Just the nave survives as the parish church, plus those distinctive towers at each end of it, reminiscent of Dr. Doolittle's double-ended friend the Push-me-pull-you. This is in fact the tale of two towers, which developed, one might say, into a towering row.

The man responsible quite unintentionally was Henry I's Chief Butler, William d'Albini. In those days a king's butler did rather more than fling open the double doors and announce dinner was served. He was virtually the King's right hand man and when the King prospered, his right hand got a fair grip of whatever was going.

D'Albini had all the right connections. He married into East Anglia's leading family the Bigods, and his son later married the King's widow. In 1107, when he decided to found a priory at Wymondham, it was very convenient that the Abbot of St Alban's happened to be his uncle.

Wymondham Abbey

In what was doubtless intended to be a generous gesture, d'Albini announced that the priory church should also serve as the parish church for the townsfolk of Wymondham. Unfortunately he failed to employ a good lawyer to tie up the details and nobody was quite clear how this arrangement was supposed to work. It was a nice idea in theory; in practice it was a recipe for disaster.

One gathers there was not too much love lost between the monks and the locals anyway. The monks on the whole were better educated, but they knew little about Norfolk people and Norfolk ways. They may not have intended it, but these newcomers were regarded by many as unwelcome outsiders. That situation may seem faintly familiar, but there was the extra irritation that the monks were able to collect money from the townspeople for the priory. It was not the happiest atmosphere for sharing a church.

It was in fact fraught with problems. Nobody was quite sure who was entitled to use which part of the church for what purpose. Being on the spot, and with ecclesiastical authority behind them, it was not surprising that the monks tried to extend their control, but the harder they tried, the more the locals resisted. What should have been just a little local difficulty reached such a pitch that in 1249 the Pope himself was asked to sort things out.

His judgement was not quite up to Solomon's standards. Basically, he allocated the nave and the north aisle to the townsfolk and the monks got the rest. At that time there were three towers, a large central one and a smaller pair at the west end of the church. Again the monks got the lion's share, the central tower and one of the smaller ones.

It all seems a bit one-sided but for a hundred years or more things muddled along. But the monks, it seems, were still not satisfied. In the early 1400s, when the central tower weakened and had to be replaced, they sited the new one further up the aisle, blocking off a quarter of its length and leaving the locals to face a blank wall and a couple of small doors into the east of the church.

While the tower was being built the monks moved their bells into one of the smaller ones – as it happened, the one which had been allocated to the parish. And as a further irritant, when they moved the bells back into their new tower, they blocked up the entrance to the one they had 'borrowed'.

It was all too much for the townsfolk. Led by their four churchwardens they blocked up the doors leading to the monks' end of the church, unblocked their tower and hung their own set of bells in it.

But they still couldn't win. The monks' bells were bigger and grander and their new tower was much higher. When the locals rang their bells for services nobody could hear them.

Things began to get out of hand. Monks were attacked in the streets and harassed during their devotions. The Prior's house was broken into and his life threatened. In spite of being bound over in huge sums of money to keep the peace the townsfolk kept up their campaign. In desperation they petitioned King Henry IV, asking for permission to replace the two small towers at the west end of the church with a much bigger one, for their bells.

The petition is now in the Abbey archives. It is written in Norman French, and after a polite start – 'We, your poor humble lieges, the inhabitants of Wymondham in the County of Norfolk' – it launches into a lengthy complaint about the monks preventing them from attending services because of the bells in their big tower. Children, it said, were dying unbaptised as a result. A new tower was urgently needed – and anything the monks could build, it implied, they could build better.

It took another 30-odd years and a new Lord of the Manor, who helped to finance the tower and negotiate with the monks, before they eventually got their way. The new tower was actually being built when the Priory became an Abbey. And since the Dissolution of the Monasteries – a popular move in Wymondham, I suspect – the monks' tower, together with their end of the church has been a ruin, while the people's tower is still in use.

Alas, for one Wymondham family its existence proved a mixed blessing. After Robert Kett and his brother William led that far more famous but less successful protest by Norfolkmen, Robert was hanged in Norwich, but William was brought back home and hanged in chains until he died – from the townsfolk's tower of Wymondham Abbey.

How Oulton acquired its chapel

A general and a pastor who chose their wives shrewdly

AT FIRST SIGHT IT LOOKS rather like a pair of unromantic semi-detached houses, with two rows of large plain windows and a door at each side. Only the roof with its twin Dutch gables indicates that it is anything out of the ordinary; and only the worn tombstones in the grass beside it give a hint of its real identity. This is Oulton Chapel, one of the oldest Non-conformist chapels in Norfolk, left to become derelict in the 1960s, now beautifully restored by the Norfolk Historic Buildings Trust.

Inside this unlikely exterior, rows of wooden pews face a magnificent pulpit, which is backed by a six-sided sounding board decorated with inlaid patterns and stars. The roof is supported by two great pillars of solid wood, complete tree-trunks that must have been erected before the chapel was built around them. A gallery runs round three walls, with more rows of pews, so that altogether the chapel can seat about 150 people. The grandest pews are at the back, each with its own door; all of them are fitted now with individual electricity sockets for heaters, a luxury most parish churches would envy. New chandeliers have been hung, but the old coke stove has been restored and the original clock, made in Aylsham, is still set in the front of the gallery, where the preacher could not avoid seeing it.

Anyone who still pictures Norfolk as a vast expanse of flat fields would never believe that this was in the same county. The chapel stands alone on a grassy hillside with woods behind and above it, looking across a little wooded valley at rolling hills, with the manse set some distance below, alongside the tiny lane that meanders off to Oulton village. There is no connection with Oulton Broad – unless you count a nearby stream, which in due course joins the Bure, and thus links up eventually with the Broad, nearly 50 miles to the south, in very different country. This Oulton is in the heart of that little-known hinterland between Norwich and the North Norfolk coast, and the village is so small and scattered that it is hardly identifiable as a village at all.

Yet Oulton has two claims to historical fame. The first dates back to Tudor times, when the local squire was one of Queen Elizabeth's judges, Sir Robert Bell. He came to an untimely end as the result of a courtroom drama that became a catastrophe. He was trying a case at Oxford Assizes, and the scurvy knaves in the dock must have been scurvier than usual, because the stench was so appalling that Sir Robert, the entire jury, the officers of the court and the spectators in the public gallery were taken ill, and all of them were dead within 50 days. Perhaps because of Sir Robert's experience judges were given a nosegay to carry – and prisoners, I hope, were given a bath.

Oulton's second distinction, of course, is the chapel. Why on earth, I wondered, was such a substantial place of worship provided in such a remote place? And where did it find a congregation? Mary Manning of the Norfolk Society has provided the answers for the Trust, and they involve a Cromwellian general who made two shrewd marriages, one to a Norfolk heiress and the other to a daughter of Cromwell.

Major-General Charles Fleetwood was in command of the Eastern Counties in 1657, and later became Commander-in-Chief. His first wife was Frances Smith, whose family owned Irmingland Hall, a few miles from Oulton, and in due course he moved in. He was a fanatical Dissenter and maintained a chapel at the Hall that no doubt all the staff and estate workers had to attend. When he died in 1692 his son Smith – confusingly, that was his Christian name – inherited the Hall and the chapel. Smith's daughter married the pastor, the Reverend Abraham Coveney, who seems to have been as shrewd in his choice of wives as the Major-General. However, he wanted to move to a chapel at Guestwick, and was very put out when the job went to someone else. 'Piqued by failure,' as Mary Manning puts it, 'Coveney moved the Irmingland congregation to Oulton and set about building a chapel there.'

She records that a small mineral spa existed near the site he chose, probably the first in Norfolk, and known locally as the Spaw; the lane from Irmingland to Oulton is still called Spaw Road. So perhaps Coveney liked to take the waters as well as services, and moved there to combine the two. Work on the chapel was completed in 1728 and it was officially opened on 1731; I am not clear why there was such a delay, but maybe the Spaw was too much of a draw...

The chapel remained in use for some 230 years, but once it was left empty it soon began to deteriorate. In 1989, when it was in a very bad way, the Norfolk Historic Buildings Trust came to the rescue.

Now there are regular open days, it is available for meetings and other activities, and it has again been used for occasional services. More recently another of its original functions has been restored, and in the twenty-first century a bride has again walked up the aisle to be married in Oulton's historic old chapel.

The hatters, the hermit and Mr Pennoyer

How a guild chapel became a village school

LOOKING AT IT FROM THE road, you might think this is just another Victorian village school, with the familiar red brick classrooms, the familiar asphalt playground and, these days, the familiar signs of disuse, which indicate that its last pupils have long since departed. Only the unusual shape of the windows in the main block, partially out of sight, give a hint to the casual passer-by that Pulham St Mary School is a little out of the ordinary.

It started life, in fact, as a medieval guild chapel. It is claimed to be the oldest primary school in the country and the County Council's leading specialist in this field, conservation officer Stephen Heywood, says it has a remarkable history 'which is rendered exceptional by the survival of a medieval chapel of considerable distinction at its core'.

Even inside it is still difficult to spot anything remarkable about it. The classrooms look like classrooms, the school cloakroom like a school cloakroom, and the school toilets – yes, those too. But the arched windows in the main block do look distinctly ecclesiastical and the walls of that block are built of flint instead of brick.

This is what remains of the original guild chapel and the confirmation can be found, of all places, in the coalhole. This was another Victorian addition, built onto the west wall. The wall has been bricked up inside and painted to look like any other kitchen wall, but on the coalhole side it remains exposed – and there, to delight the eye of any passing coalman, is the splendid medieval archway that once framed the west door, decorated with the carved pre-Tudor roses that the local preservation committee now uses as its logo.

Perhaps the earliest person to walk through it was not a coalman but a Colman – Walter Colman, first custodian of the newly built guild chapel of St James the Greater, back in 1401. St James is the patron saint of Spain, whose relics, they say, were miraculously conveyed to Spain from Jerusalem in a ship made of marble. When a knight saw it sailing into port he was understandably startled, and so was his horse, which plunged into the sea. Unlike the marble ship the horse failed to float, but the knight managed to climb aboard. He found his clothes covered in scallop shells – and they have been the saint's emblem ever since.

The school at Pulham St Mary

None of this seems to have much connection with Pulham St Mary, but in fact St James the Greater had a lesser role, as patron saint of the Guild of Hatters, Cappers and Hurers, and it just so happened that Pulham had quite a large community of hatters. When they decided to build a new guild chapel separate from the church, they dedicated it to their patron saint, and installed Walter Colman as the resident hermit.

It would be nice to think that Walter was the earliest recorded ancestor of the present Lord Lieutenant, but alas, there is no evidence of any connection and as Walter presumably led a celibate life, it is doubtful he had any descendants.

There is no doubt, however, of his name. In 1401 the Bishop of Ely granted 'forty days of indulgence' to anyone who helped to have the chapel built and contributed to the support of Walter Colman, 'the poor hermit there'. Incidentally, 40 days of indulgence did not mean a licence to swill; it just meant spending 40 fewer days in purgatory. It was a less tangible reward – but Walter got their donations anyway.

The Guild chapel continued to function for the benefit of local members until Edward VI, emulating his father, suppressed the guilds and confiscated their properties. The chapel disappeared from the record books for more than a century, until it featured in the 1670 will of William Pennoyer.

Mr Pennoyer was actually born William Butler, but his father Robert, a Herefordshire man, changed the family name when he moved to Bristol. 'He happened to be present where a man was killed,' hinted one cryptic report. Pennoyer was a common name across the Welsh border but why Robert picked it is still unexplained. I like to think that one day some painstaking genealogist will come across a note saying: 'I chose Pennoyer, just to annoy'yer...'

Young William kept the name and in due course went to London to make his fortune as a cloth merchant, sugar importer, arms dealer and general entrepreneur. His full story is told in the excellent *History of Pennoyer's School* by the local historian, Hilary Clutten.

Pennoyer was as shrewd in investing money as he was in making it. Like a good Puritan he spent very little of it on himself and at his death he left numerous bequests to educational charities and other good causes. They ranged from Cambridge College in Connecticut, later Harvard University, to the village school at Pulham St Mary.

It might seem odd for this tiny Norfolk village to feature in the will of a merchant who was born in Herefordshire, brought up in Bristol and spent the rest of his life in London, but one of his many lucrative investments was a fifteenth share in the Manor of Pulham, where he also bought a number of properties, though he never lived in them. But he must have taken his responsibilities seriously as a fractional Lord of the Manor and in his will he left the profits from this fifteenth share to provide for a free school in Pulham St Mary in the guild chapel. Pennoyer's School existed there for over 300 years until its closure, through falling numbers of pupils, in 1988.

Since then the village has tried to preserve the building and find a new use for it, and I am sure that Walter the Hermit would be glad to know that his old home has not been forgotten.

The rector who moved Edgefield church

'What hills of difficulty, what valleys of depression
I went through...'

IF YOU WERE ASKED TO name Norfolk's most remarkable village parson
your thoughts might range from the diary-writing James Woodforde
of Weston Longville to the hapless Harold Davidson, Rector of Stiffkey,
though my friends in Dereham would doubtless plump – and what
an apt word that is – for the lovably rotund and slightly eccentric Canon
Noel Boston, expert on antique firearms, who was wont to illustrate
his talks in the 1950s by living up to his office and firing a miniature
cannon. He is the only speaker I can recall who was able to keep
Dereham Rotary Club fully awake after lunch.

However, Norfolk has produced another cleric with an even more
spectacular achievement to his credit. Canon Walter Marcon, Rector
of Edgefield for over 60 years, decided when he took over the parish
in 1875 that the church he was responsible for occupied an
inconvenient site away from the village – so he moved it!

Just moving house, so they say, can be as traumatic an experience as
getting married or getting divorced. Moving church – and literally at
that – presents even greater problems, and Canon Marcon admitted
in his little book, 'The Translation of a Church', that at times he felt
discouraged. Well, that's putting it mildly.

'What joys, what sorrows, what hopes and fears, what hills of
difficulty, what valleys of depression I went through ...' Yes, he makes
his point. However, he reminded himself of how Nehemiah rebuilt
Jerusalem and managed to take a philosophical view.

'Every man from Nehemiah downwards knows that if he is going to do a good work there will be some to hinder and frustrate him,' he wrote. 'So many people will today oppose a thing which tomorrow they will welcome. Giving women the vote is a case in point.' I wonder if he would say the same about ordaining them?

The old church of St Peter and St Paul was built about the 13th Century in what was then the centre of the village, in a valley handy for water from the River Glaven. But like so many Norfolk villages, Edgefield was ravaged by the Black Death in 1349, and the few survivors moved out of their contaminated homes and built new ones on high ground about a mile away.

Edgefield Church today

For the next five hundred years they trooped back into the valley every Sunday for their church services, but that wasn't good enough for the new young Rector. Actually he wasn't new to Edgefield; he was born in the Rectory, and as a lad he had trekked up and down the hill to church with everyone else, but now he was in a position to do something about it – particularly as the church was in such an appalling state that it seemed almost as easy to move it as to restore it where it was.

'Its broken and moss-covered walls, its miserable seating, its chancel arch with a threatening bend in it, the wretched altar old and stained, its font with only its Early English bowl remaining, without pedestal or foot space, were enough to try the stoutest heart,' he wrote – and many other rural Rectors must know how he felt.

So he held a parish meeting, got the agreement of those present and applied for a faculty to move the church. But inevitably there were dissentients and a quite inaccurate rumour was spread that graves and headstones would be damaged in the process. Few things arouse the passions of Norfolk villagers more than the thought of a tombstone being tampered with, and written objection was sent to the Bishop. However, according to the Rector, many of the signatories were not villagers who belonged to the church, and several of the signatures were in the same handwriting. They had also forgotten to give a name and address to reply to –'an omission it was not my business to rectify,' observed the Rector dryly. The faculty was granted.

The Marchioness of Lothian, who lived at Blickling Hall, presented him with a convenient new site for the church and he was able to launch his Removal Appeal. An uncle started him off with £100, he managed to contribute £800 himself, partly by taking in pupils, and in due course he reached his target of £2,000. In 1882 the work began.

'Bit by bit the roofs were taken down, the walls slowly razed to the ground, the wrought stones were marked so as to ensure each stone going in his proper place again adjoining his fellows above or below, then brought up and laid out on the grass in their own patterns…'

Only the chancel and tower were left behind and the tower still stands on its original site in the valley, next to a farmyard. The medieval rood screen and parclose screen, the monuments on the walls, and the oldest item of all, the font bowl, were reinstated in the rebuilt church. It was consecrated by the Bishop of Norwich on 14th July 1884 – but it was still without a tower.

The Rector resumed his money-raising but it was not until 1909 that the tower was completed, and he was still a hundred pounds short. 'I was in despair about it when Mr Charles Page – God rest his soul – sent me a cheque for that amount. My family tell me that I danced about the room, waving the blessed piece of paper as if I had taken leave of my senses!'

So the translation of the church was complete and this remarkable country parson was able to enjoy the fruits of his labours until he died in 1937, in the same room at the Rectory where he was born. In 1984 a stained-glass window was installed in the church to mark the centenary of its consecration. Featured in the window is Canon Marcon himself, in his long black cassock and little round hat, riding his old boneshaker bicycle on his way to a service. For me it is a reminder that few people have managed to reduce their mileage to work in such an enterprising fashion as the man who moved Edgefield Church.

Jacob and Billy, the images on the Image Barn

And the furious farmer who put them there

DRIVING ALONG THE ROAD BETWEEN Guist and Melton Constable, I must have passed the 'Image Barn' scores of times and never noticed anything unusual about it except that, with its crow-stepped gables matching the farmhouse a few yards away, it is a very handsome barn. I may have registered that there was an object of some sort on top of each gable, but I probably assumed it was just another weathervane. Norfolk farmers do tend to put up weathervanes on their barns, since the weather has such an important bearing on their livelihood – and more often than not, the vane is decorated with the figure of a man with a gun, or a dog, or both, because shooting is almost as important to most of them as the weather.

But the figures on the 'Image Barn' at Wood Norton are not part of a weathervane and they have no guns and no dogs. It so happens though, that one of them has a pheasant beside it and both are certainly connected in rather a different way with shooting.

The figures are actually busts of real people. The one which has the pheasant is inscribed Jacob, and is an effigy of Sir Jacob Astley of Melton Constable Hall, later Lord Hastings. The other, which holds a law-book, was named Billy, short for William Norris, squire of Wood Norton. They were put there not as a mark of esteem, but as a mocking gesture by the man who owned the farm, in order to annoy them as they drove past in their carriages – the road was the direct route between their homes.

There have been various versions of the story behind these effigies, and indeed it has been linked with quite a different barn on the Hastings estate that happens to have one of those shooting-orientated weathervanes on the roof. But thanks to some friends who live in Wood Norton, I have a copy of the notes made about the Norris family by William Norris, Billy's great-nephew, and they include the definitive version of 'The Image Barn Incident'.

Image Barn

Billy Norris was born in 1797 and inherited his father's estates in Wood Norton and Guist in 1835. According to his great-nephew he was quite a character. For instance, he recounts the story of his mother's visit to Wood Norton Hall, when Billy said she must meet his new housekeeper. He sent for her, but when she arrived he told her first to go outside and stand on the grass opposite the front door. 'Then,' writes William, as if he were planning where to plant some trees, he told her 'A little more to your right, thank you...' When he was satisfied with her position, he told her approvingly, 'If ever they grow like you, woman, they will make fine trees.' Only then, it seems did he remember to introduce her. William comments frankly: 'From the foregoing and many other tales told of him, it will be seen that the Old Squire, as he was called, was eccentric.'

In spite of that, or perhaps because of it, Billy Norris was the chairman of the Reepham Bench, and it was in that capacity that he found himself immortalised on top of the 'Image Barn'. The farmer who lived there, described by William Norris simply as 'Mr Phillips, a Socialist', came to the help of a defendant, presumably a friend or employee, who had been accused of poaching by Sir Jacob Astley. Sir Jacob's gamekeeper had found a pheasant in a trap, hid nearby to see who would remove it, and arrested this man.

The lawyer engaged by Mr Phillips claimed that the gamekeeper had put the pheasant in the trap and the defendant had been tempted to take it, but Billy Norris and his fellow magistrates, not surprisingly, were unconvinced. The man was duly convicted.

'Phillips was so angry at the conviction,' writes William Norris, 'that he pilloried the prosecutor and the chairman of the Bench by putting their effigies on a new barn he was building, close to the road along which 'Billy' and 'Jacob' constantly passed to visit each other's houses. Sir Jacob was furious, but William took all his friends to see it!'

This reaction seems well in character for Billy Norris, an eccentric himself at heart who remained so until his death. In 1875 he was taken ill at his holiday house in Torquay and was told he had three days to live. He sent for Stone, his coachman and factotum, and gave him detailed instructions. His body was to be taken by train to Ryburgh station, an undertaker from Dereham called Page was to meet it and convey it to Wood Norton Hall, and there the coffin was to be put through a window into the dining room. 'On the day of the funeral,'

Billy instructed, 'the corpse will be taken out through the hall – but be very careful of the corner, it is very awkward.' William Norris adds in parenthesis: 'It still is'.

Billy also told Stone that he must walk alongside the hearse, not ride on it, from Ryburgh station to Wood Norton, some three or four miles. Unfortunately it poured with rain all the way, and the driver of the hearse, no doubt very wet himself and hoping to get along a bit quicker, urged him to climb aboard. But Stone kept trudging along the muddy road. 'No.' he said, 'Master wouldn't like that.'

The Old Squire bequeathed the estate to his great-nephew William, who made his home at Wood Norton until his death in 1934, leaving behind this splendid family archive. His widow, however, sold both the Hall and the estate, thus ending a family link with the village that went back many generations. But Billy Norris lives on at Wood Norton, perched on the roof of the 'Image Barn'. Time and the weather have blurred his features but I like to imagine that, however Mr Phillips originally portrayed him, he is actually having a jolly good chuckle.

A pub with a Bible in the bar

Customers could 'refresh the mind as well as the body'

TAKING THE LORD'S WORD INTO public houses is generally associated with the Salvation Army and their energetic distribution of the 'War Cry', but a mid-19th century Norfolk curate was there ahead of them. He not only took it into his local pub, he left it there for the permanent benefit of the customers, a very large church Bible – and happily it is there still, albeit in a glass case these days, in the bar of the Crown at Banningham. They still call it the Curate's Bible and it must be quite a rare feature to find in a village inn.

I did come across another pub in Cumbria where a big old Victorian family bible is kept permanently in its own little cupboard in the bar, but nobody seemed quite sure why. There was supposed to be a clause in the deeds which forbade its removal from the premises, but the current landlord said he had never seen it, though he agreed the Bible was part of the fixtures and fittings and he would never dream of moving it. An inscription showed it had belonged to a family called Wood, presumably former tenants, and it contained a record of their births, marriages and deaths up to the first World War, but much as I would like to believe it was left there for the instruction and education of future customers, I suspect they actually just forgot it when they moved out.

The Curate's Bible, on the other hand, was put there for a very specific purpose and it is not tucked away in a cupboard. The curate, who presented it to the Banningham Crown, just across the road from St Botolph's Church, left a very clear message on the flyleaf. The Revd. E.H. Bickersteth wrote that he was giving it to the pub 'on the condition it is placed in the public room, in the greatest hope and prayer that he who calls there may read the Word of God and find salvation and refreshment of the mind as well as the body.'

As a guide for new readers he added a few pungent quotations from the Bible 'to help you overcome the Evil One'. Appropriately, they are mostly of a sobering nature. 'The soul that sinneth, it shall die,' he warns. 'Whosoever shall keep the whole law and yet offend in one point, he is guilty of all.'

The Bible was either greatly used, or greatly maltreated, in the years that followed. The original flyleaf is missing. Many of the pages are torn and tattered, and the edges have been stained a deep yellowy-brown, the sort of colour found on the ceilings and walls of pubs before the lung cancer era.

Happily the book has now been rebound and it is safely protected in its glass case. The lid can be removed but the barman was slightly shocked when I took it out. Casual dipping into its surviving pages is discouraged, and unfortunately I can understand why. On one of the few blank pages, the one that separates the Old and New Testaments, a gentleman called G.D.Whitear, of Garden Street, Cromer, has kindly recorded his name and address for posterity. That was back in July 1953, and Mr Whitear may now be deceased, but if he still resides in Garden Street, how tempting to go and write one's name and address on his front gate…

In more recent times the customers of the Crown have appreciated the Curate's Bible rather more, including Mr Christopher Pipe (also of Cromer, but no other connection), who first told me about it. 'I have never been able to make up my mind,' he wrote, 'whether Bickersteth was just being over-optimistic in thinking people would read the Bible over their pints, or whether people really did do that in those days. Perhaps they adjourned from the morning service to the pub and argued over the sermon, so he thought they needed a Bible to refer to, to settle their arguments?'. A nice thought, Mr Pipe, but perhaps just a Pipedream…

As for the curate who presented the Bible, he went on to greater things. Having served at St. Botolph's Church for three years in the late 1840's, he moved onwards and upwards through the church hierarchy, and became Bishop of Exeter in 1885. He retired 15 years later at the age of 75.

Bishop Bickersteth was a hymn writer of some repute, and his best known is still included in the hymn books: 'Peace, perfect peace, in this dark world of sin.' The bar of the Crown Inn is not exactly a dark world of sin, but the Curate's Bible, now patched up and protected inside its glass case, after years of rough handling, is enjoying a little peace as well.

High drama at Binham Priory

A siege, a king to the rescue, and a workman falling off the roof

I HAVE TO SAY THAT at first sight, Binham Priory is not one of Norfolk's most elegant ecclesiastical buildings. As you approach it from the village, the great block of south wall with its diminutive windows and low-pitched roof looks more like a warehouse than a church, and when you enter the farmyard which serves as the car park, you are confronted by that vast bricked-up window in the west front, which makes it look as though the place has long since been abandoned. It has a blank white circle in one side like an empty eye-socket, giving the impression that what remains of this once majestic building is trying to turn a blind eye to the indignities inflicted upon it over the centuries. The tiny bell-cote perched above it, with its solitary bell, seems slightly embarrassed at being involved in all this; it would look much happier, one feels, on the roof of the village school.

Nevertheless the Priory Church of St Mary and the Holy Cross is reckoned alongside Castle Acre as one of the great historical treasures of Norfolk architecture. Certainly it has one of the longest histories. When William the Conqueror distributed chunks of what he had conquered to his friends and relations, his nephew Peter de Valoines must have drawn a short straw; he found himself in Binham, in the bleak and windswept wastes of East Anglia. Perhaps for want of anything else to do, he founded a Benedictine priory there in 1091, an off-shoot of St Alban's Abbey. The St Alban's monks must have regarded this as a posting to be avoided, and the Abbot may have taken a similar view, because he made it an official rule that an Abbot could only stay at Binham Priory for eight days in a year.

It took more than 150 years to complete the building of the Priory and it took Henry VIII only a few months to knock most of it down, but that original date, 1091, is the one that counts. So in 1991 the 900th anniversary was celebrated with such a memorable pageant and son-et-lumiere that in Binham they talk about it still. And for me it was a great way to learn about the history of this remarkable building.

Binham Priory, of course, has certain advantages over the average parish church for this sort of thing. The scale of it is rather different for a start. The present church is just the nave of the original one; there was a chancel and transepts and a presbytery, surmounted by a splendid tower that would have made the little bell-cote feel even more uncomfortable. There were cloisters, the prior's lodging, the refectory and dormitory and guesthouse, a tithe barn and watermill and fishponds – the facilities were a little more lavish than the average church hall, and the hospitality after Sunday morning service was not limited to a thermos of coffee at the back of the church. That has all gone now, but the space remains a marvellous setting for a pageant.

Binham has some famous figures in its history like Prior Richard de Parco, who built that astonishing west window and would be pretty sick to know that its fine geometrical tracery fell into such disrepair that it was replaced in 1809 by a solid mass of red brick. He would also be no friend of Sir Thomas Paston, who was given the site when Henry VIII dissolved the monasteries, and made a useful profit from it by demolishing parts of the priory and selling off the rubble to builders; difficult to picture the illustrious Pastons as builders' merchants...

The pageant recreated the most famous event in the village's history, the siege of the Priory by Robert FitzWalter in 1212. FitzWalter was friendly with a Prior who was sacked by the Abbot of St Alban's. To get him his job back, he produced a forged document saying he was patron of the priory, and laid siege to it. The monks, it is said, were forced to eat bran and drink water from the drainpipes. The actors probably baulked at that, but we certainly saw King John on horseback, leading his troops to the rescue with the famous exhortation: 'By God's feet, either I or Fitzwalter must be King of England'.

Other parishes may not have the experience or the manpower to stage that kind of spectacle, but I am sure most of them can match another scene in the Binham pageant, literally the high spot, in which a workman falls from the roof of the church after meeting the ghost of mad Alexander de Langley. True, we may not all have an Alexander de Langley, the Prior of Wymondham who went mad through over-study and was kept in solitary confinement at Binham until his death. But I bet that a great many workmen have fallen off a great many churches in Norfolk through the centuries, and it should not be too difficult to find a ghost to tie in with them. The real problem, I suppose, is to find someone to play the part, but certainly the Binham workman was, one might say, the hit of the show – and happily survived to take a bow.

Similarly, other parishes may not have had a visit from King John at the head of his troops – though actually the Binham church guide says he *sent* an armed force there, so it may be stretching a point. But with Sandringham so handy, few parishes cannot claim a royal connection of some sort, if it was only a wave as they drove by, and others have had royal visits long before Sandringham. I remember a pageant at North Elmham in the 'Fifties, when Charles I strode majestically through Elmham Park, resplendent in long dark wig and large feathered hat. I have no idea why such an elegant and sophisticated monarch should wish to visit deepest rural Norfolk – perhaps the pageant organiser just happened to acquire a long dark wig and a large feathered hat – but who is to say that he didn't? I have to say this is my kind of history…

The legacies of two eccentric Victorians

A garden in a chalk pit and Spanish names in rural Norfolk

THE NAMES OF ROBERT HARVEY and Henry Trevor may be unfamiliar to most of us now, but in the 19th century they each left their own permanent marks on Norfolk, in most unusual ways.

General Sir Robert John Harvey, Lord of the Manor of Tharston in south Norfolk, was Wellington's right-hand man in the Peninsular War, and when he retired he changed the map of the county by giving the farms and roads on his estate the names of the battles he fought in, and the officers who fought with him.

Meanwhile in Norwich Henry Trevor, shopkeeper and cabinetmaker, left behind him not only his furnishing firm of Trevor, Page & Co, which survived until the 1970s, but also the astonishing Plantation Garden in Earlham Road, described by Sir Roy Strong as one of the city's great surprises – 'a horticultural treasure... in many ways over the top.'

Although their lives overlapped, it is unlikely their paths ever crossed. The general was very much 'County', Henry was very much 'Trade'. The difference was emphasised in the advertisement for Henry's first shop in 1842:

'In opening the above establishment,' said the *Norwich Mercury*, 'H. Trevor begs most respectfully to solicit the attention of the Nobility, Clergy, Gentry and Public in general to a useful stock of the Newest Design...'

Sir Robert probably qualified both as 'Nobility' and 'Gentry', but I suspect he was far too busy re-organising and re-naming his estates to drop into H. Trevor's for the odd fireside chair.

I am not sure how much the average farm worker knew about the Peninsular War in the early 1800s; I confess my own knowledge of it was never profound. My only lasting memory is a line or two I learned at school from Charles Wolfe's famous poem about the burial of Sir John Moore at Corunna, when without any sound or a funeral note, out to the ramparts they hurried. 'We buried him darkly at dead of night, The sods with our bayonets turning...'

But I had little idea what Sir John was doing at Corunna, or indeed where Corunna was. And on the Harvey estates in Tharston, Forncett and Stoke Holy Cross, they must have been a bit bewildered when the farms they had known all their lives by their local names were re-christened Torres Vedras, or Salamanca, or Ciudad Rodrigo.

Plantation Gardens, Norwich

However, perhaps I underestimate the General. Perhaps when he rewrote the maps he schooled his tenants in the history and significance of the strange-sounding places in which they now lived.

He may have explained, for instance, that Torres Vedras formed part of the British defence line from the Portuguese coast to the River Tagus. And that Salamanca was the scene of a famous victory over the French, and Ciudad Rodrigo was where his colleague General Picton rallied his troops with the cry: 'It is not my intention to spend any powder this evening, we'll do this business with cold steel' – which explains why, in Tharston, there is not only a Ciudad Rodrigo but also a Picton Farm.

General Harvey's personal role in the war is described on the splendid memorial to him in Tharston Church, guarded by the figures of two soldiers in the uniform of the period. He was 'the principal organ of communication' between Wellington and the Portuguese troops who were defending their country alongside the British. 'He was near his Grace's person in all operations and engagements with the enemy,'

Henry Trevor would not have enjoyed that role at all. He was a strict Baptist, devoted to his church, his family, his good works – and his business. He was only 22 when he opened his first shop in Post Office Street. Within ten years he was employing 30 people. When he died, a hundred employees attended his funeral.

He invested in property as well as trade. When he acquired nearly three acres of land on the Earlham Road he not only built the Plantation House for his own family but also another substantial house for rent in a corner of the grounds, which is now the Beeches Hotel. Then he added the terrace of seven houses alongside his grounds that still stand in Chester Place. The rents on his properties provided a handsome supplement to the profit on his furnishing business.

Surprisingly, the site he chose for his Plantation Garden was actually a chalk quarry, right beside the city gaol. But over the years he transformed it into a quite remarkable example of Victorian landscape gardening, and by a happy chance – or did this shrewd businessman have some prior knowledge? – the city gaol was demolished and replaced by a rather more prestigious neighbour, the Roman Catholic Cathedral.

In recent years, the Plantation Garden Preservation Trust has largely restored Henry's creation to its original condition, complete with its Italianate terrace and Gothic fountain, its rustic grotto and its imitation medieval wall. Whatever style came into fashion, Henry went for it.

To complete the restoration a replica of the original rustic bridge was constructed from old photographs with the help of the Norwich Society, and it was formally opened – by me, as it happened – as part of their 75th anniversary celebrations.

I had just been visiting Tharston Church with its Harvey memorial, and for me the bridge helped to span the gap between two slightly eccentric Victorians. One planted an exotic garden in a chalk pit, the other planted exotic names from the Peninsula in the Norfolk countryside. Perhaps the shades of Henry Trevor and General Sir Robert Harvey sometimes meet on that rustic bridge after the rest of us have gone – and share a quiet chuckle over the unlikely legacies they left behind.

Chapter four

Legends and traditions: Some are just memories, others still live on

England's only Episcopal wherry

The Bishop's annual visit to St Benet's Abbey

THERE IS A TIME OF year when certain villages in other parts of the country go gently and rather charmingly dotty. At Grasmere in Cumbria, for instance, children dress up as 'rush maidens' in green and white dresses with flowers in their hair, and carry a sheet full of rushes to the church – even though they haven't been used as a floor covering since 1841. At West Witton in Yorkshire they 'burn the bartle', a straw-filled effigy representing a thief who stole a pig on St Bartholomew's day. At Youlgreave and many other Derbyshire villages they have revived the pagan practice of putting flowers on wells (and pumps and water tanks and even taps) to placate the water gods. And so on…

But here alas, we seem to miss out on these jolly eccentricities. There is a map of folklore and customs in Britain that shows Norfolk as almost completely blank. It just records the ancient fairs at Norwich, Downham Market and King's Lynn. Another map showing 'folk heroes' is even emptier. So is a map of 'ceremonial dances', though I have seen some enthusiastic Morris men in the west of the county.

However, there is one ancient ceremony this month that has been successfully preserved over the centuries and is unique to Norfolk. If there were a map of Britain showing 'traditional Episcopal wherry processions' it would surely have just the one dot, in the middle of the Norfolk Broads. On the first Sunday in August, the Bishop of Norwich, in his other capacity as Abbot of St Benet's, sails along the Bure to take the annual service in the ruins of the Abbey.

Everyone who has been on the Broads must be familiar with the ruined gatehouse of St Benet's and the stump of the mill that was built inside it, long before the protective days of English Heritage. But the early history of the Abbey, and its link with the Bishop of Norwich, is perhaps less well known; indeed even the experts seem to differ at times.

Some say there was a Christian hermitage on the site as early as 690 AD, and the first monastery was founded by the Benedictines about a hundred years later. Everyone seems to agree that King Canute then became involved, after his invasion of Britain in 1016, but some historians make him the hero, others suggest he is partly the villain.

The heroic version is that the monastery was destroyed during the much earlier Danish invasion of 870 AD, and Canute rebuilt it as an act of repentance for the behaviour of his forebears. But it is also said that Canute himself burned down the monastery. Then, in a remarkably quick change of heart, he rebuilt it on a more lavish scale, pardoned the Abbot for trying to defend it against him, and allowed the monks to return.

This curious love-hate relationship between the attacker and the attacked seems to have been repeated when a later invader, William of Normandy, sent his forces to capture St Benet's. The siege lasted four months and then his general devised the sort of cunning plan that would have appealed to Captain Blackadder. He sent a soldier under a flag of truce to demand the Abbot's surrender, but as well as the flag the soldier carried a note which he slipped to the monk on the gate, inviting him to a secret talk with the general.

Like King Canute, the monk is sometimes portrayed as a hero, albeit a naïve one, and sometimes a villain. His detractors say he betrayed his fellow monks in order to be made Abbot. But the pro-monk lobby say he saved their lives and risked his own, by doing a deal with the general on their behalf; if he had refused, the general would have slaughtered them all.

Either way, the result was the same. That night the monk opened the gates, and the Normans took the Abbey. But then comes the love-hate relationship between visitors and vanquished. The general fulfilled his promise to install the monk as Abbot 'for life' – then hanged him from the bell tower, reinstated the original Abbot and allowed the monks to resume their duties.

It was not until the days of Henry VIII that the Abbey finally succumbed, when the reigning Abbot became Bishop of Norwich; he surrendered the Cathedral's properties to the Crown while being allowed to keep those of St Benet's. The Bishop still holds both offices, hence the annual service.

According to legend the hanging of the monk took place on May 25th, and in other parts of the country they might well have commemorated the event on the lines of 'Burning the Bartle'. But in this case 'Anging the Abbot'. Instead we celebrate, in a rather more civilised fashion, the historic link between the Abbey and the Bishop.

The procession has had its unplanned moments. Bishop Peter Nott recorded one in his 1996 'Pilgrimage Diary', when he sailed with Peter Bower in the wherry 'Hathor':

'After years of sailing on the wherries once or twice a year,' he wrote, 'Peter now allows me to steer, which is great fun. But when I think I'm doing rather well he never fails to remind me of a disastrous occasion on Wroxham Broad, when I was steering and we accidentally jibed and headed straight for the pristine landing stage of the Yacht Club. It took three of us straining on the heavy tiller to avoid a major catastrophe!'

This time they arrived without incident, but he noted another unexpected moment after the service. A lady took his photograph and said she would put it next to her picture of the Pope. 'Ecumenical breakthrough', I thought. But the new Roman Catholic Bishop of East Anglia is also called Peter, so maybe it was a case of mistaken identity…'

On his return journey he took the helm again on '*Hathor*' and managed some rather tricky tacking. He recorded Peter Bower's guarded congratulations. 'You did that quite well, but don't go round telling people you can now tack a wherry. Remember Wroxham Broad!'

I am sure he will, along with all the other high spots of his years in Norfolk – not least his annual pilgrimage as Abbot of St Benet's. And I know he will remember them with affection – just as we shall remember him.

'Religious, grave and discreet'

The scarlet-cloaked ladies of Castle Rising

THERE IS AN OLD ADAGE they used to quote in West Norfolk:

> *'Rising was a seaport when Lynn was but a marsh,*
> *Now Lynn is a seaport town and Rising fares the worse.'*

Until the fifteenth century Castle Rising was the main port of entry for West Norfolk, from the time when St Felix sailed up the Babingley River to bring Christianity to East Anglia in 630AD. Then the river started to silt up, the sea started to recede, and although there was still a tidal harbour for another couple of hundred years, it couldn't cope with the big ships, which were getting bigger all the time.

While the water level at Rising was falling, at King's Lynn it was rising. The merchants took their ships to the deeper harbour, just as centuries later the Norfolk Line was to forsake Yarmouth for Felixstowe, and Castle Rising was left, one might say, high and dry.

But thanks to the loss of its sea trade Castle Rising has remained comparatively undisturbed; and in spite of its historical importance from its days as a Norman stronghold, its delights remain largely undiscovered.

The village has not entirely escaped attention, but most visitors come to see the castle ruins and long may this distract them from the village centre itself, which lies off the road behind the church, well away from the English Heritage direction signs.

The church is almost as notable as the castle, but Norfolk is full of notable churches and for me the main delight of Castle Rising is the secluded green with its splendid trees and imposing memorial, the fine old houses just visible beyond mellow walls and elegant gateways, and finest of all, the Hospital of the Most Holy and Undivided Trinity.

This is West Norfolk's answer to the Great Hospital in Norwich, a group of historic dwellings where elderly folk can live out their days in comfort and peace. The man who built it in 1614 was Henry Howard, Earl of Northampton, whose family was given the Castle Rising estate by Henry VIII.

He founded four of these 'hospitals', and each one was a reminder of how his relations were deeply embroiled in the politics of state, generally with disastrous results.

He dedicated the hospital at Castle Rising to his grandfather, the third Duke of Norfolk, who was imprisoned by Henry VIII and only escaped execution because the king died on the day before it was due to be carried out. A hospital at Greenwich was in memory of the Duke's son, Henry Howard's father, who was not so lucky over his execution – the king died the day *after*. A third hospital at Clun in Shropshire commemorates Henry's brother Thomas, the fourth Duke, who was beheaded by Queen Elizabeth. There is a hospital unconnected with incarcerations or decapitations at Shotesham, his birthplace, but even that had unhappy associations because his parents were on the run at the time from the king.

Henry himself fared rather better. He too fell out of favour with his cousin Queen Elizabeth I, but Kipling would be glad to know he kept his head while all about him were losing theirs, and survived to enjoy the patronage of James I. Perhaps in thanksgiving he went into the hospital construction business, and in the case of Castle Rising, never was £451.14s. 2d better spent. It has served its original purpose and retained its unique traditions ever since.

The buildings themselves are impressive enough, ranged around a courtyard that you enter through a gateway flanked by twin towers and capped by turrets. But the buildings would be nothing without the 'sisters' who live in them, twelve elderly ladies who have to be 'of honest life and conversation, religious, grave and discreet, able to read if such a one be had, a single woman, her place to be void on marriage, to be 56 years of age at least, no common beggar, harlot, scold, drunkard, haunter of taverns, inns and almshouses.' Having met the present incumbents I am sure these conditions are still being strictly observed – though one sweet old lady did suggest, after I had taken up much of her time with my camera, that I owed her a gin-and-tonic.

But they are used to cameras, for a very good reason. Another condition Henry Howard laid upon them was that they should attend church in special cloaks and hats, rather like the traditional Welsh costume, only more so. The cloaks are a splendid scarlet, embroidered with the Howard crest, and the hats are quite astonishing affairs, tall and black and conical, and while the Welsh version is flat at the top, these come to a point.

The ladies still parade across to church in this garb, led by the Matron, who has a rather dashing cloak with a three-tiered cape and a much more manageable tricorn hat, trimmed with a black ostrich-feather. The general effect is reminiscent of Margaret Lockwood in her Wicked Lady gear, leading a procession of benevolent witches. The scene, as they cross the quiet tree-lined lane between the hospital and the church, can't have changed much since the days of Henry Howard, and it's another reason for Castle Rising being thankful that the North Sea left it high and dry. After all, I don't fancy those old ladies' chances trying to cross the road to church in the middle of King's Lynn.

No, the writer of that old couplet may reckon that 'Rising fared the worse', but I would offer this postscript:

'Now much of Lynn is modernised, a place for the go-getter,
And I'd say, in the long run, Castle Rising's fared the better.'

Pub games – an endangered species?

Long live pitchpenny and the Norfolk Twister

IT IS ONE OF THE sadder facts of life these days that, due partly to the drink-driving laws but largely to the ludicrous price of draught beer, the only way many pubs can stay solvent is to become restaurants with bars.

In Norfolk, as in other rural areas, you often find that the tables on which the locals used to play dominoes and draughts are now laid with knives and forks. The dartboard has been replaced with a blackboard giving 'Today's Specials'.

Any attempt to play a game of dice on the bar – quite a common practice a few years ago – can attract glares from nearby lunchers irritated by the noise, and frequently has to be suspended while a menu-clutching customer leans over to question the landlord on the calorie content of the lasagne. In some pubs the bias is so much in favour of eaters rather than drinkers that you can feel terribly conspicuous just standing at the bar holding a drink, while everyone else is sitting at a table tucking into gammon, egg and chips.

I should not complain because I enjoy a good pub lunch myself. The food is generally cheaper than in a restaurant, the standard of cooking is often surprisingly high, and nobody expects a tip. But I do mourn the resulting disappearance of the traditional pub games. Most skittle alleys have long since gone anyway, to make space for pool tables and fruit machines, but it seems there is not even room for a shove ha'penny board. I did find one pub in Suffolk with a table marked out in squares for a game called quigleys – but nobody could remember how to play it, so I was having my lunch on it. And when did you last see a game of Nine Men's Morris, that entertaining combination of draughts and noughts-and-crosses, which according to Dr Brewer's Dictionary of Phrase and Fable, is 'an ancient game once popular with shepherds and still found in East Anglia'? Alas, I have yet to find it. What I have found, however, and I have rejoiced at each discovery, are two little-known Norfolk pub games which have become quite rare over the years, but still manage to survive in the Age of the Pub Lunch. One of them actually bears a Norfolk name, though I have to admit it is not unique to this county. It crops up elsewhere under a different pseudonym, but to me it will always be the Norfolk Twister.

My first discovery, however, was made some years ago, in the days when the Lifeboat Inn at Thornham, on the North Norfolk Coast, was still a fairly basic local pub. It is reputed to have once been the haunt of smugglers, as indeed is every pub anywhere near the coast, but in the case of the Lifeboat one could quite believe it.

Not any more. In recent years a large extension has been built to provide overnight accommodation and it has become a major catering operation. But mercifully the original public bar still remains, with its old wooden settles and battered tables, though the tables are now laden with cod and chips and the settles are occupied by hungry hikers. However, the Morris Men still dance occasionally in the lane outside, and inside there is still the traditional game of pitchpenny, or as some counties call it, toad in the hole.

It consists of a hole in the seat of a settle, reminiscent of a commode except that for all practical purposes except pitchpenny, the hole is far too small. The Lifeboat retains thirteen pre-decimal pennies and the object of the game is of course to toss all the pennies into the hole. Only one player in the last forty years has done it, and I was once assured that a gallon of whisky awaits the next – though in these changing times the prize has probably been altered to a free dinner for two…

I have attempted this feat myself and three pennies was the maximum. But I hope that other customers will continue to ask for a go and encourage the landlord to preserve this reminder of less food-orientated days. I have come upon pitchpenny since in Essex and Kent, but is there another, I wonder, here in Norfolk?

My second discovery was much more recent, in a pub which I have visited more than once but I had never noticed it before; perhaps I was too busy ordering my pub lunch. On my last visit to the Three Horseshoes at Warham, however, which is still an unspoilt village pub with beer served from the barrel, I happened to glance upwards at the ceiling, and saw what looked like an inverted roulette wheel. A circle about eighteen inches across, divided into twelve red and white segments with a pointer in the middle.

This, I learned, was a Norfolk Twister, a traditional pub game presumably designed for tall players with long arms. They spin the pointer on the ceiling and bet on which segment it will stop in – not very demanding on the intellect perhaps, but a genuine old pub game nonetheless, which can still be played even if the tables set around the walls are being used for rabbit pies and local shrimps and baked crab in cheese sauce (they do cook excellent bar food at the Three Horseshoes).

The Norfolk Twister may have survived elsewhere in the county. According to a note written in 1948 there were four in Norfolk, but the chances of their survival seems remote. I would be delighted to learn that I am wrong.

As I said, the Norfolk Twister is not as Norfolk as all that. I found a very similar device in a pub near the Sussex coast, where they called it the Spinning Jenny. It was supposed to have been used by smugglers to decide how they should split up their spoils – which is as good a tale as any other smuggling story. But I do not begrudge it to them, far from it. I treasure all the pitchpennies and the Norfolk Twisters, wherever they may be, as examples of how traditional pub games can survive in an era when the only game in a pub can be in a pheasant sandwich.

The many fresh starts of the Lynn Mart

From St Nicholas to St Valentine via January and June

WHEN THE CROWDS GATHER IN the Tuesday Market at King's Lynn to hear the Proclamation of the Mart – 'Whereas by Royal Charter and Prescription, the Mayor and Councillors of the Borough are empowered to have and to hold in perpetuity, one Mart or Fair yearly on the fourteenth day of February and for six days thenceforth next and immediately following…' – they might well assume, in view of the date, that the Mart has something to do with St Valentine, the Roman martyr whose day this is, and whose name is forever associated with pierced hearts and chubby cupids.

Actually there is no connection at all. Nor for that matter, is there any connection between St Valentine and Valentine cards. It is more likely that the custom of making amorous advances to one's beloved, albeit anonymously, is linked with the mating season of birds which just happens to start around this date.

Certainly Chaucer thought so: 'For this was on St Valentine's Day, When ev'ry fowle cometh to choose her mate.' And so did Shakespeare: 'Good morrow, friends. St Valentine is past, begin these woodbirds but to couple now?' (Shakespeare always preferred the earthy approach.) It was much later that greetings card manufacturers spotted a gap in the market.

The Lynn Mart marks the start of the showmen's touring season rather than the woodbirds' mating season, and it was originally on quite a different date – in fact, different dates, because for quite a time there were two Marts a year.

King John started them off in 1203, when King's Lynn was still Bishop's Lynn. Even before he granted the town its first charter he gave the Bishop of Norwich, as lord of the town, the right to hold a fair on the

Feast of the Translation of St Nicholas, May 9th. Again there seems no connection between the fair and the saint.

After King John splashed off across the Wash, the date of the fair was juggled around among a curious assortment of saints. St Margaret, as patron saint of the town, quite logically acquired it first, on the vigil of her feast day, July 20th, but in the 1280s, for no obvious reason, it was switched to August 1st, the feast of St Peter AD Vincula.

A couple of centuries later Edward IV decided to grant the Bishop an extra fair in Lynn and changed the dates yet again. One was to start on January 13th, the feast of St Hilary, the other on June 1st, the feast day of two little-known Saxon saints, St Wistan and St Wite. None of them seems to have much connection with hoopla stalls.

Having fun at the Lynn Mart

King Edward must have been a good friend of the Bishop – who no doubt got a cut of the fair's profits – because he not only doubled the number of them but as an extra bonus he extended their duration from 15 days to 40.

Henry VIII, no great lover of Catholic bishops, soon changed all that. He granted letters patent to the Mayor and the burgesses to hold fairs instead of the bishop, cut them down to seven days, and switched the dates yet again, this time to coincide with the two feasts associated with the Virgin Mary, her Purification on February 2nd and her Assumption on August 15th. Just to make sure everyone appreciated how times had changed, Bishop's Lynn became King's Lynn.

Unfortunately King Henry did not check his Showmen's Diary before fixing these dates. He should have realised that August 15th was slap in the middle of the Mart season. In particular it clashed with the great fairs at Ely and Stowbridge. Business slumped, confusion reigned, tempers rose.

It was Good Queen Bess who sorted things out. In 1559 an Act of Parliament was passed, pointing out the clash of dates in the summer and confirming only the winter Mart on February 2nd. And it would still be held on that date, were it not for an enormous hiccup in the English calendar in the 18th century.

Other countries had changed their calendars nearly 200 years earlier, when Pope Gregory decreed that the old Julian calendar had got out of kilter over the centuries, and 11 days had to be lost to put things right. Britain, characteristically, stayed out of step with her European neighbours, but being 11 days behind everyone else must have been very irritating for exporters, tourist operators and visiting football teams, and we eventually came into line.

The Government announced in 1752 that September 2nd would be followed by September 14th, thus creating new problems. For instance: should ancient customs be observed on their traditional days, or according to the new calendar?

In King's Lynn they reached a typical Norfolk solution. The Feast of the Purification was still celebrated on the same date, February 2nd – but the Lynn Mart was moved to February 14th. So it was goodbye to the Virgin Mary, hello St Valentine – neither of whom could have been too bothered – and thus it has remained ever since.

Incidentally, when the Mayor takes the traditional opening ride on the roundabout (it is only when none is available that he goes on the dodgems) I wonder if he or she recalls the much earlier Mayor who invented it. In 1885 a young Lynn engineer called Frederick Savage, who had already invented a winnowing machine took out a patent for his 'galloping horses'. When he became Mayor, I hope that at his installation the entire Council joined him on his 'gallopers'. There is, after all, nothing too unusual about a local authority going round in circles...

The art of taking a knap

Forget the Flintstones, here's the real thing

A TERRACE OF OLD COTTAGES in the next village has been extended by a new one on the end. There were considerable misgivings locally when this was proposed because the existing cottages are flint and it seemed unlikely the new walls would match, but the result is not bad at all.

The new flints are more uniform than the old ones because 150 years ago they used all shapes and sizes for farm cottages, some split, others put in whole. At a casual glance, though, the effect is perfectly acceptable, and in a year or two it should be difficult to see the join.

This use of flints seems to be getting popular again amongst builders and I suspect it is not entirely for aesthetic reasons. The whole of West Norfolk sits on a vast belt of flint-bearing chalk, and the building material is there for digging. Modern builders are rediscovering what the Romans knew, that flint is as good as stone or brick when you are putting up a wall, so long as it is built a layer at a time and the mortar allowed to harden before the next layer is added. These days, with a lining of breeze-blocks behind it, you don't even have to worry about that. It also has the benefit of needing virtually no maintenance – not for a hundred years or so, anyway. There are still some Roman walls at places like Caister-by-Yarmouth and Burgh Castle, up to 15 feet high in places, so that new terraced cottage should see most of us out.

The best known source of flint in Norfolk doesn't function any more, but as it's 4000 years old that's hardly surprising. Incomers can be confused by its name, Grime's Graves; they are liable to enquire who Mr Grime was and why he needed so many graves. Actually these pits were thought to be burial places until some shrewd Victorian archaeologist – a Mr Grime, perhaps? – correctly identified them in 1870 as ancient flint workings, an important production centre for Neolithic man, the Sheffield of Stone Age Britain.

The first miners were only one step on from Cave Men. They used picks made from antlers of the red deer that roamed the forest and they dug these pits to reach the best-quality 'floorstone' flints, about 40 feet down. They made galleries to dig out the flints, and during their lunch breaks they made drawings in the chalk with their antler picks. Both the drawings and antlers are still there, and one or two of the antlers still have fingerprints preserved in the chalky paste on the handles.

It didn't occur to these early miners, however, to use the flints for building. They mainly wanted them as axe heads to chop down the trees which grew in such profusion in Norfolk, and also of course to thump each other with when tree-felling got too boring. It took the Romans to see their real potential.

The flints used by the Saxons and Normans were just picked up in fields or taken from pits dug near the building sites; Grime's Graves, presumably, were already out of action. But in the Middle Ages serious flint-mining returned to Norfolk at Lingheath, not far from the original workings and in the 16th century they discovered a new market for their product. The cores of the flints were still sold to builders, but the flakes chipped off them, previously just thrown away, went to the makers of all those newfangled flint-lock guns. The demand continued for another 300 years, then came cigarette lighters, but they're not quite the same…

The builders meanwhile were developing more upmarket methods with their flints. Instead of using them whole, or chipping them into a convenient size, they went in for knapping. The flints were chipped into rectangles so they could be laid in straight courses, like bricks.

This 'flushwork' is still found all over Norfolk, but these days I know of only one full-time flint knapper – and when I last met him he was being kept so busy that he had to divide his time between four different sites. As there is no modern equivalent of Grime's Graves he also has to tour the chalk and lime quarries, where flints are normally considered a rather useless by-product, to get his supplies. So it wasn't easy to catch him knapping, as it were.

When I did, though, it was a fascinating process to watch. He sat on an old chair with a pad strapped to his knee, rested a flint on it, tapped it quite gently with a hammer, and split it in just the right place. I asked him how he knew where to hit, and he said it was just a matter of angles, and tried to explain, but in fact there is no real explanation. He just knows.

Only one face of the split flint, the face that is exposed, is chipped into a rectangle; the rest is left rough to bind into the mortar. Even so, it is a laborious process – his production rate is about two flints a minute. I remember when I met him he was doing the decorative front wall of a house in Saham Toney, near Watton. It wasn't a very big wall, but when I met him in January he had been working on it for three months, and hoped to get it finished by Easter.

That was some years ago, and I haven't come across him since but I hope he is still roaming the Norfolk countryside, as his predecessors did so long ago, a happy wanderer preserving an ancient skill – and of course his knappersack on his back...

When the saints come marching in

Walstan, William, Withburga – and Wandregesilus

'For all the saints, who from their labours rest…'

WE SHOULD SING THIS ROUSING hymn with particular fervour in Norfolk because we do have quite a notable selection of local saints. One thinks of St Walstan, the eleventh century prince's son who laboured in the fields all his life, finding God among the furrows. His shrine at Bawburgh attracted pilgrims for hundreds of years. There was St William of Norwich, the boy saint said to have been crucified by the Jews, though in terms of saintliness Norwich is famous more for Mother Julian, the 14th century mystic, than poor young William.

It is the story of St Withburga of Dereham though, that I find the most fascinating. A story of skulduggery as well as saintliness, and just the sort of characters to feature in a television mini-series: a beautiful heroine, a wicked bailiff, marauding Danes, an infamous abbot and ruthless monks. For animal lovers there are even a couple of pet deer. All that it lacks is a handsome hero, but these rarely feature in stories of women saints, or perhaps the women would not have stayed so saintly.

The basic plot is well known. Withburga was the daughter of Anna, the confusingly named King of the Angles. She founded a nunnery at Dereham, was saved from starvation by the appearance of two does which supplied her with milk, evaded the attentions of an unpleasant bailiff, and lived a blameless life until she died, full of good works. Her shrine became such a popular place for pilgrimage that the covetous Abbot of Ely decided to steal her body to divert the pilgrims – and their gifts – to his own Abbey. He had the slender excuse that her sister Etheldreda, who founded the Abbey, was buried there already and could do with her company. After he and his monks had removed the body, a holy well appeared on the site of her tomb, and the pilgrims continued to come, while at Ely her new resting place was neglected and eventually forgotten. Not quite a happy ending, perhaps, but a touch of poetic justice.

Even without any embellishments it should bring a sparkle to a television producer's eye, but plenty of extra colour has been added over the centuries. There is more about the wicked bailiff, for example, who disapproved of Withburga's free milk supply and came to hunt the deer; the scene is depicted on Dereham's town sign.

The holy well of Withburga at Dereham

Then there are the Danes, who turned up two centuries after Withburga's death and burned down the church and most of the town, though amazingly they left her tomb intact. And most dramatic of all, there is the theft of the body a century later by the Abbot of Ely, who came to Dereham with his monks, plied the townsfolk with food and drink to render them comatose, then disinterred the body and made a night-time departure.

There have been many imaginative versions of all this, notably by a 19th century Vicar of Dereham, the Rev. Benjamin Armstrong, who describes in remarkable detail what happened when the theft was discovered:

'Every man, woman and child in Dereham was roused and ran shrieking to the empty tomb in the church, and at the sound of a horn, all the people from all the hamlets near unto the pleasant hill of Dereham came trooping in with bills and staves... When they saw or were told about the empty tomb, the people all shouted: 'Who hath done this deed? Who hath stolen the body of our saint?"

Which is not a bad quote after nine centuries, but another colourful touch is added by Ben Norton in his *Story of East Dereham*.

'Although she had been dead nearly 300 years, the virgin princess with all her clothing was as fresh as ever and her limbs flexible, and so bashful was she at being looked at by the men, that when one of the monks ventured to touch her flesh, a rosy blush suffused her cheeks.'

Definitely a six-part series, with Sharon Stone as St Withburga and Antony Hopkins as the Abbot...

As well as our local saints I should mention an 'adopted' one whom most chroniclers miss. St Wandregesilus, or Wandrede for short, lived during the seventh century in what is now France. He was a noble courtier who went off to be a monk, but the king disapproved and ordered him to return. On his way to the palace he stopped to help a carter haul his horse out of the mud, and arrived very late and distinctly grubby. When he explained, however, the king forgave him and sent him speedily on his way – if only to avoid getting any more mud on the carpet.

There is no evidence that Wandrede ever visited Norfolk. Instead he spent ten solitary years in the Jura mountains – 'Wandrede lonely as a cloud' perhaps? – then founded a monastery near Rouen, where he died. But when the Bailiff of Norwich in 1272 built the little parish church of Bixley, a few miles outside the city, he dedicated it to this obscure French abbot; it is believed to be the only church in England that bears his name.

The Bailiff never explained his French connection, but I can only think he had some special affinity with the saint. Maybe he was born under a Wandrede star...

The original Jack the giantkiller?

But Tom Hickathrift was a fair size himself

NORFOLK IS NOT PARTICULARLY RENOWNED for producing extremely large people and I used to assume there had only been one Norfolk giant, the redoubtable Robert Hales, a farmer's son from West Somerton who was seven feet eight inches tall and weighed 32 stone. He made a useful living by touring fairgrounds in Britain and America before taking over a London Pub, where his formidable size not only attracted inquisitive customers but also ensured their good behaviour. He died in 1863 and lies beneath a suitably imposing monument in West Somerton churchyard.

There is, however, another contestant for the Norfolk Beefy Stakes who lived, worked and ultimately died in West Norfolk, and he performed his most famous feat near Tilney All Saints – a feat which some say provided the basis for the immortal tale of Jack the giantkiller.

Tom Hickathrift, originally from the Wisbech area, was certainly a giantkiller but he was no stripling himself. He lived in the days of William the Conqueror, so nobody can be quite certain of his size – the Doomsday Book did not record the measurements of local inhabitants – but he was already six feet tall by the time he was ten, with all the muscles to go with it. Nobody appreciated just how powerful those muscles were, until his mother sent him to fetch some straw and the unwary farmer said he could take as much as he could carry. Tom gathered together enough straw to fill a wagon, tied it up in one enormous bundle and carried it home.

Mrs Hickathrift, no doubt realising she was on to a good thing, sent him back for another load. Again the farmer said he could take what he could carry, but this time, so the story goes, the cunning fellow hid two enormous rocks in the straw. Young Tom merely wrapped up the rocks with the straw and carried away the lot. As an extra twist to the story, when the rocks fell out of the bundle on the way home, Tom is said to have merely shrugged and commented: 'How badly they have cleaned this straw, there are still grains of corn dropping out' – but I think that is pushing it a bit, even for a legend.

Tom was supposed to be a fairly dim sort of fellow but I can't help thinking he was brighter than he appeared. When he was told, for instance, that he could carry home some firewood in payment for a day's work, he uprooted a fair-sized tree and took it away on his shoulder. When he moved to King's Lynn to work for a local brewer, who told him (very injudiciously for a Norfolk man) he could drink as much as he liked, he nearly drank the brewery dry. But his employer decided to keep him on, since he could lift five times as many barrels as anyone else, and Tom was given the regular job of delivering beer from King's Lynn to Wisbech.

The direct route was only a dozen miles but unfortunately it offered an even greater hazard in those days than the current traffic on the A47. Part of it ran through territory belonging to a local giant, who took the view that trespassers should be prosecuted, then beheaded. He didn't actually say 'Fee fi fo fum', but he certainly fancied the blood of an Englishman

Tom was either stupid enough not to care, or shrewd enough to know he stood a fighting chance. Fed up with taking the long route around the giant's territory and emboldened perhaps by his remarkable daily beer intake, he decided one day to take the short cut – and immediately met the giant. There was then an exchange between the two burly fellows which has gained a rather unlikely elegance down the centuries. It went, apparently, as follows:

Giant (irritated): 'Sirrah! Who gave you authority to come this way? Dost thou not see how many heads hang on yonder tree, that have offended my laws? Thine shall hang above all.'

Tom (intoxicated): 'Who cares for you? You shall not find me like one of them.'

Giant (infuriated): 'Why, you are but a fool, if you come to fight me and bring no weapon to defend yourself.' He then produced a very large club and prepared to thump the daring drayman into a pulp.

But once again Tom proved he was shrewder than he looked. He took a wheel off his cart to act as a shield, and in the other hand he used the axle as a stave. In no time at all he beat the giant to the ground, and with a touch of poetic justice he knocked the giant's head off his shoulders. It is not recorded whether he hung it up with the rest.

Like Jack the giantkiller, Tom returned from this violent encounter much richer than when he left – the giant's cave was full of gold and silver, 'Daft Tom' became Mr Hickathrift and went on to achieve many more notable victories – not least, vanquishing the Devil in the churchyard of Walpole St Peter – before gaining well-earned retirement.

Opinions differ as to how he spent it. The up-market version, is that Tom Hickathrift was knighted and became a governor of Thanet, but others say he set up home with a tinker who was the only man he ever met whose fighting abilities matched his own. No doubt the tabloid Press would read something significant into this rather bizarre liaison, and take the legend a step further…

As for actual evidence of Tom Hickathrift's existence, there is a muscular effigy flexing its pectorals in Walpole St Peter which might well be Big Tom, and two or three ancient stone crosses in the Terrington and Tilney areas are known as Hickathrift's Candlesticks, though it is not clear why. Over the county border, I gather, the Wisbech area has a Hickathrift Farm and Hickathrift Corner.

But the best bet, in my view, is an outsize coffin lid nearly eight feet long in Tilney All Saints' church, which is said by some people to have marked his grave. I have to admit that most Norfolk guidebooks suggest the coffin belonged to Sir Frederick Tilney, who was killed at the Battle of Acre – but with great respect to Norfolk guidebooks, I know which theory I prefer.

How the salesman's cross saved Bromholm

Was the double crucifix genuine or just a double cross?

EACH YEAR IN SEPTEMBER THE church celebrates Holy Rood Day, the Feast of the Exaltation of the Cross on September 14th, when the True Cross was returned to Calvary in 629AD.

But pieces of the Holy Rood continued to circulate for many centuries after that; indeed, if all the pieces had been genuine, the Cross must have been as lofty as St Paul's. But one piece, which found its way to Norfolk early in the 13th century, seems to have been the real thing, because it brought healing to thousands of pilgrims – and a wave of prosperity to Bromholm Priory.

There is little left now of the Priory, just a gateway and a few ruined walls not far from the Bacton gas terminal, and during the last war its ancient stonework was ignominiously stuffed with chunks of concrete for use as a defence post. But in medieval times it rivalled Walsingham as one of the great holy places of Europe – and all because of this tiny piece of wood.

Bromholm was founded as a Cluniac house in 1113, an obscure and remote little priory in a remote and obscure corner of East Anglia, and it stayed that way for 100 years, struggling to make ends meet. Then along came a travelling salesman, an itinerant priest who offered them his 'bargain of the week', a little double crucifix which he claimed was carved from the True Cross – and he had all the sales patter to go with it.

He was, he said, a former chaplain to the Bishop of Constantinople and in the course of his duties he had acquired this relic, which he guaranteed genuine. He may not have mentioned that he had already tried to sell it to the monks of St Albans, together with two of the fingers of St. Margaret of Antioch. They had bought St Margaret's relic – they apparently had no objection to being offered two fingers – but they had turned down the double crucifix. They may have been suspicious of a double cross...

At Bromholm, however, the monks had more faith – or perhaps they were just more gullible. They had a whip-round, delved into their modest coffers and bought the double crucifix. It was the turning point of their lives.

The cross was found by St Helena 300 years after the Crucifixion, buried beneath the heathen temples that had been built on Calvary. The remains of three crosses were uncovered, so it is said, but the finders shrewdly tested each of them on a sick woman and the one which healed her was declared the True Cross.

Helena had it placed in a silver shrine inside the church she built on the site, but she was not above keeping a substantial chunk for herself back home in Rome.

Did the Bromholm Cross come from that piece, or from the Cross she left behind, or from one of the other two, which could loosely be described as a cross of Calvary? Or was it just a fake, but the monks had such faith that it was enough to perform miracles?

We shall never know, but we do know about the miracles, or what seemed to be miracles to those who saw and recorded them. Thirty-nine people were brought back to life, lepers were healed, the lame walked, the blind could see...

In no time at all, pilgrims were pouring in from all over Europe. Chaucer gave a helping had by publicising the Bromholm relic in *The Canterbury Tales*: 'Help, Holy Cross of Bromholm,' the Miller's Wife exclaimed. Piers Plowman gave it a plug too: 'Bid the Rood of Bromholm bring me out of debt,' he pleaded. It received the royal seal of approval when Henry III made a pilgrimage to Bromholm in 1233, when he was still a young man. It obviously did him good; he continued to reign for another forty odd years – quite a feat in those turbulent times – and lived until he was 65, then considered a ripe old age.

Bromholm was still going strong a couple of centuries after Henry's visit, because it was chosen as the burial place for the distinguished John Paston, by his wife Margaret, of *Paston Letters* fame. Margaret was utterly devoted to her husband, as the letters illustrate. How's this for instance, for a handsome apology:

'Right worshipful husband, I recommend me to you, beseeching you that ye be not displeased with me, though my simpleness cause for you to be displeased with me. By my troth, it is not my will neither to do nor say that should cause for you to be displeased; and if I have done, I am sorry therefore and will amend it. Wherefore I beseech you to forgive me, for your displeasure should be too heavy for me to endure with...'

Any other wife would have just said 'sorry'.

As you would expect from such devotion, Margaret wanted only the best for her husband's last resting-place and chose Bromholm – though his remains were later transferred to Paston. It is recorded that at his splendid funeral at the Priory, 'the reek of the torches of the dirge was so overpowering that the priory glazier had to remove two panes of glass so that the mourners should not be suffocated.'

Thus the travelling salesman's piece of the Holy Rood kept Bromholm Priory in Rood health, as it were, for at least 200 years. But priories fell out of favour and in due course more than two panes of glass were removed and Bromholm was reduced to the ruin that remains today. As for that precious piece of the Holy Rood, who can say where it went? Perhaps Holyrood House in Edinburgh knows the answer.

Tie another legend round the old oak tree

From Robert Kett to some old cobblers

TO MOST OF US IN Norfolk the name Robert Kett is associated with Kett's Rebellion, which began in 1549 with a march from Wymondham to Norwich in protest against the illegal enclosure of common land. It ended some six weeks later when the Earl of Warwick arrived from London with 12,000 trained soldiers, routed Kett's followers and executed hundreds of them in various unpleasant ways, including Kett himself, who was hanged at Norwich Castle.

But I always associate him with oaks. He seemed to spend a great deal of time either sitting beneath them, marching past them, or assembling his followers around them.

I suppose the most famous of Kett's Oaks was the one that stood on Mousehold Heath, replaced in later years by a rather less romantic water tower. 'The Tree of Reformation', as it was also known, had a covering in its branches to form a kind of open-fronted tent, and it served as Kett's courtroom as well as his military headquarters while he camped outside the city.

Here he dispensed justice to oppressive landowners who were brought before him by his supporters – and according to most historians his justice was a lot fairer than the treatment which he and his men eventually received from the Earl of Warwick.

Another of Kett's Oaks is at Hethersett on the road from Wymondham to Norwich, and it is reasonable to assume that Kett's men rested beneath it on their march to the city. But a Kett's Oak at Ryston is not so easy to explain, because Ryston is in the far west of Norfolk, near Denver, and a long way off Kett's route. Arther Mee, however, in his well-known guide to the county, is in no doubt about it. He agrees that many other oaks are associated with Kett 'because his followers were believed to have met under them', but adds firmly, 'Ryston's Oak, still vigorous, is authentic.'

The rebellion did attract support from various parts of Norfolk, and it is quite possible that a contingent came from Ryston, but it would be an interesting coincidence if they decided to assemble under an oak tree – particularly as it stood in the park of the Lord of the Manor, who would hardly have made them welcome.

It has definitely been established that volunteers came from Castle Rising, also in West Norfolk, and they might have had a Kett's Oak too, but unfortunately they chose an old earthwork for their rendezvous, so the village has a 'Kett's Castle' instead.

From small acorns...

Once you start looking for notable oaks in Norfolk you find that Robert Kett did not have a monopoly of them. The Tharston Oaks, for example, have been referred to by a succession of writers over the centuries, and one tree in particular was described in 1833 as 'an extraordinary oak tree, supposed to be at least 500 years old.'

Unfortunately it was burnt out some 40 years ago; it is thought that either local children or a chilly tramp lit a fire inside the hollow trunk. But the other oaks still stand, and as they are on private land the local farmer kindly took me across the fields to see them. The undergrowth is now quite dense around them, but they rise above it most imposingly, their long gnarled branches still extending across a substantial area.

Norfolk oaks have caught the eye of artists as well. John Crome, for instance, founder member of the Norwich School of Painting, took a fancy to an oak at Poringland, and in due course Crome's Oak earned a place in the National Gallery.

But I think my favourite is one which has also been preserved on canvas, though the artist may not be quite so renowned. It was not only very ancient, but it had a remarkable career. At various times it served as a cobbler's shop and as a pigsty, before it had to be felled in 1860 to avoid it collapsing. When it was carted away, the whole village turned out to bid it farewell, and since 1919 the site of the Bale Oak has been under the protection of the National Trust.

The oak used to stand outside Bale church, and a painting inside All Saints gives a vivid idea of how it looked in its final years. It resembles in fact a gorgon's head, with twisted branches instead of serpents for its hair, the stumps of two branches for its bulbous eyes and a hole in the trunk for its open mouth.

The painting also features reminders of the curious uses to which the old hollow tree was put. Cobbler's tools indicate the presence of the shoemaker, and a pig symbolises its use as a 'swine sty'. The cobbler, the swineherd and the pigs are all depicted inside the tree on the village sign, which stands beside the Bale Oak's successors outside the church.

In Arthur Mee's time there were 21 oaks 'rising as high as the church tower' and forming a spinney that is still called the Bale Oak. Today there are only a dozen, comprising one of the smallest areas of National Trust woodland in the country.

The original oak might well have been the oldest in Norfolk. A notice on the site says categorically that it had been there for a thousand years, which would make it even older than the church. Indeed the inscription under the painting in All Saints says it was probably a sacred tree in pagan times. In that case the Bale Oak would certainly qualify as a marker for one of those mysterious ley lines which some say are a source of latent energy. Perhaps if Kett's Oak on Mousehold Heath had been on a ley line too, that rebellion might have had a very different ending.

Weird wells – with a body thrown in

No wonder some of them are petrifying – literally

THIS IS THE STORY, one might say, of three holes in the ground – and I can hear you joining in the response from your childhood: 'Well, well, well…' That indeed is what they are, but each one had its own strange tale to tell. There are various ways in which wells can acquire an unusual reputation. Here in Norfolk we are very strong on wells connected with saints – St Withburga's at Dereham, for example, and St Walstan's at Bawburgh.

But wells can also have much more sinister associations. Sometimes they are linked with ghosts and dead bodies. Others are supposed to contain buried treasure. And there are 'petrifying wells' which can turn objects to stone. Happily, Norfolk has examples of all three.

Around 1800, Happisburgh had a well with a body, at a spot called Well Corner. It seems the village was regularly haunted by a legless ghost – without legs that is, not just very drunk. I am not sure how it managed to move around in this condition, but perhaps it had two wooden legs and a good sense of balance. It was further hampered by the position of its head, which hung down its back. Nevertheless, when two local farmers decided to follow it one night, the ghost led them unerringly to Well Corner.

It threw into the well a bundle it was carrying – it did have a full complement of hands and arms – then managed to jump in after it. So, understandably curious, the farmers returned next morning to search the well.

Sure enough, it contained the legless body of a sailor; the missing legs, still wearing boots, were found inside the bundle. The sailor was assumed to be a smuggler who had fallen foul of his comrades and been murdered.

Unlike the standard storybook ghost which has its head tucked underneath its arm, it would seem that this one haunted Happisburgh carrying its legs...

This kind of story rarely leaves any concrete evidence behind, but the tale of the Callow Pit Coffer could be the exception. It has been told in Southwood, near Reedham, for at least a hundred years, and may date back much further, to the time when a great flood devastated the village in 1606.

There was reputed to be a coffer of gold in the pit, perhaps left behind by some local worthy as he fled from the floods. He may well have been deterred from retrieving it by the headless horseman that patrolled the crossroads where the pit lies.

However, two sturdy locals with the same spirit of adventure as those two Happisburgh farmers, decided to search the pit for the sunken treasure. (Some versions call it a well, but Callow Pit is definitely a pit these days – maybe that flood made all the difference.)

They rigged up a platform over it and started fishing – and like their counterparts in Happisburgh, their boldness paid off. They hauled out a chest and hoisted it onto the platform by putting a pole through the ring on the lid.

Then they detected a smell of sulphur – never a good sign when buried treasure in involved. Suddenly a black arm emerged from the pit, grabbed the chest and disappeared with it, back into the murky water. All that remained was the ring from the lid, still dangling on the pole. That ring, according to the story, survived as evidence; the men took it with them and hung it on the door of Southwood church.

In 1881 the church was allowed to become derelict, and it is now just an ivy-covered ruin. But happily, the evidence of the Callow Pit treasure was preserved. The ring from the chest now hangs on another church door – St Botolph's, in the neighbouring village of Limpenhoe. If you have a good sniff, you may still detect a faint whiff of sulphur.

I suppose some unkind sceptics may suggest that the evidence of what looks uncommonly like an ordinary door-handle is not entirely convincing. However, there can be no dispute about the authenticity of Deopham's petrifying well. It is Norfolk's answer to the famous Dropping Well at Knaresborough in North Yorkshire, where the high limestone content of the water forms a stone-like coating on any object dropped in it.

There is not just one well at Deopham (near Hingham), but at least three. They are close by Crown Farmhouse, and Mr and Mrs Peter Morton, who have lived there for 40 years or more, are very familiar with the scaling effects of the local water on their kettles and pipes – or they were, until they installed a water softener.

These days the wells are covered over, and the water supply comes from the mains, but the locals still talk of the way twigs and other small objects which fall into the ditches in that area become coated with this stone-like substance.

There used to be a venerable old lime tree near the farmhouse, just beside one of these ditches, and according to local legend it got the blame for giving the water its power to 'petrify'; perhaps they saw a link between lime tree and lime-scale. It is thought to have been blown down in a gale in 1713, but in recent years Mr Morton has preserved its memory by planting another lime tree along the line of the same ditch – which is now piped in.

But as he points out, the tree was hardly to blame. The heavily impregnated water actually comes from about 300 feet below ground level, forced up by considerable pressure through cracks and faults in the earth.

Those locals at Happisburgh's Well Corner and Southwoods's Callow Pit may have felt 'petrified' at what they saw, but in Deopham's wells it's the real thing.

The many legends of King Edmund

From landing at Hunstanton to dying at Hoxne
– or was it Hellesdon?

HUNSTANTON MAY LOOK AS IF its history only goes back to Victorian times, and indeed there were only a couple of cottages there until the Le Strange family of Old Hunstanton built what is now the Golden Lion Hotel and created a 'new town' around it. But its full name is Hunstanton St Edmund, and near the lighthouse on its famous striped cliffs there is St Edmund's Point, where according to legend – and that phrase crops up constantly in connection with Edmund – he came ashore as a lad of 14 in 855 AD to claim the throne of East Anglia.

The only tangible evidence that remains is the ruined archway of a chapel on the cliffs, built more than four centuries later by the monks of Bury St Edmunds to commemorate the landing. They could only have been guessing at the precise spot, of course, and in recent times some experts have rubbished the whole story anyway, but it is worth giving it a second look.

I am tempted to start, 'Once upon a time', but 'according to legend' sounds less fanciful. According to legend, then, the childless King Offa of East Anglia went on a pilgrimage to the Holy Land to seek heavenly guidance about a successor to the throne. But he solved the problem before he even got there. He stopped for some days with his relative, Prince Alkmund of Saxony, and he was so taken with Alkmund's courteous and studious young son Edmund that he immediately earmarked him as a likely heir.

He was not aware that – according to legend – Edmund had been destined for something like this since birth. A sorceress had prophesied that the baby would attain great distinction and eventually worldwide fame.

It was just as well that Offa made such an instant decision, because he was taken ill on his way back from the Holy Land and never saw his home again. On his deathbed he told his nobles that young Edmund, 'that elegant and accomplished prince', should be the next king. A few centuries later this would probably have started a civil war, but it seems there were no objections and they conveyed his wishes to Alkmund, who mentally congratulated the sorceress on her forecast and sent his son off to East Anglia.

They intended to sail up the Waveney to Thetford, East Anglia's main centre, but – according to legend – a strong southerly wind blew them past the estuary and then conveniently became an easterly wind as they rounded Cromer and blew them along the coast to Hunstanton.

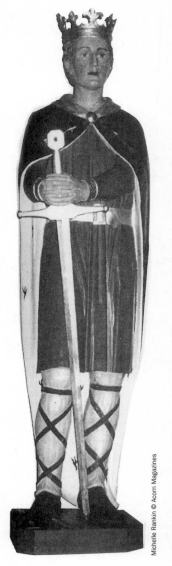

Michelle Rankin © Acorn Magazines

St Edmund, Patron Saint of Hunstanton

Edmund knelt to give thanks after he came ashore near some springs of sweet water, and – according to legend – the place was named Hunstanton after 'honey', signifying sweetness and strength. Unfortunately most experts on place names would say the real origin is 'Hunstan's enclosure' – Hunstan's-tun – and indeed some historians argue that East Anglia never had a king called Offa and Edmund came from Kent, not Germany. But the legend soon gets back on firmer ground.

Most people seem to agree that Edmund spent a year in preparation and study and even learned all the Psalms by heart, a useful accomplishment I suppose for an early Christian king. On Christmas Day 856, when he was still only 15 he was crowned and anointed King of East Anglia by Bishop Humbert at Bures in Suffolk.

A Danish prince – according to legend – was wrecked on the Norfolk coast, near a royal lodge at Reedham where Edmund was staying. The King entertained him with his usual courtesy, and they tried a spot of falconry. The visitor proved more expert at the sport than the local champion, Beorn the royal falconer, who very unsportingly murdered him in revenge. As a punishment Beorn was set adrift in the Danish prince's boat without rudder, sail or provisions, which would normally have meant certain death.

However, the boat drifted all the way to the Danish coast, where it was of course recognised and Beorn was asked a lot of embarrassing questions. He turned out to be, one might say, a Beorn liar. He admitted killing the prince but said Edmund had ordered him to do so. Hence the invasion of East Anglia, the battle near Thetford and Edmund's surrender. Refusing to renounce his faith and accept a pagan overlord, he was tied to a tree, beaten and scourged, pierced with many arrows and finally beheaded. The story may have gained an extra arrow or two along the way but the essence of it is clear.

What is not clear is where it happened. According to yet another legend it was at Heglisdune, which has been interpreted as Hoxne, but some say it is Hellesdon, and others discount Heglisdune altogether and go for Sutton Hoo down in Suffolk.

My money is still on Hoxne, largely because of the additional legend that Edmund's hiding-place under a bridge was given away by a courting couple who saw his spurs glistening, and it is still considered unlucky for newly-weds to cross the present bridge on that site.

The Edmund legends did not end with his death. There is the well-known story of how a wolf guarded Edmund's severed head from the attack of a ravenous bird – the Viking emblem was a raven – until a search party came by, when the head helpfully shouted 'Over here!' Years later Edmund's ghost rebuked the Danish King Sweyn for ravaging his land and smote him with his ghostly spear, so that on the morrow he died.

So on St Edmund's Day we should give thanks, not only for his martyrdom, but for all those splendid stories that have come down to us, many of which are illustrated in the windows of Hunstanton church. The date he died was November 20th 870 – according to legend...

Index

Index Pages with photographs are in *italics*